Letters
to My
Younger
Queer
Self

Letters to My Younger Queer Self

Letters to My Younger Queer Self

Inspiring, influential voices from the LGBTQIA+ community

Daniel Harding

HarperCollins*Publishers*

HarperCollins*Publishers*
1 London Bridge Street
London SE1 9GF

www.harpercollins.co.uk

HarperCollins*Publishers*
Macken House, 39/40 Mayor Street Upper
Dublin 1, D01 C9W8, Ireland

First published by HarperCollins*Publishers* 2025

10 9 8 7 6 5 4 3 2 1

© Daniel Harding 2025

Daniel Harding asserts the moral right to be identified as the author of this work

A catalogue record of this book is available from the British Library

ISBN 978-0-00-868506-5

Printed and bound in the UK using 100% renewable electricity at
CPI Group (UK) Ltd

All rights reserved. No part of this publication may be reproduced, stored in a retrieval system, or transmitted, in any form or by any means, electronic, mechanical, photocopying, recording or otherwise, without the prior written permission of the publishers.

Without limiting the author's and publisher's exclusive rights, any unauthorised use of this publication to train generative artificial intelligence (AI) technologies is expressly prohibited. HarperCollins also exercise their rights under Article 4(3) of the Digital Single Market Directive 2019/790 and expressly reserve this publication from the text and data mining exception.

This book is produced from FSC™ certified paper and other controlled sources to ensure responsible forest management.

For more information visit: www.harpercollins.co.uk/green

To my nan.

You loved a postcard, three rings to say that we were home safe and, most importantly, me. All of me, even without truly understanding who I was, or my own letter, G, in the queer alphabet of life. In a rainbow full of people who all deserve to be seen.

Thank you, Nan. You inspired me more than you could ever know.

We all deserve a moment feeling big in a world that often makes us small.
We all need that unconditional support – wherever it comes.
We all deserve our letter.
Our place.
This is for every one of us.
All of our letters.
None should be banned.

'To send a letter is a good way to go somewhere without moving anything but your heart.'

Phyllis Theroux

Dear Reader ...

... have you ever sat down to a desk, felt inspired and grabbed a pen? Have you ever stared in the mirror and paused for a moment, studying who you have become? Have you ever taken a moment to acknowledge the battles you have fought and the distances you have travelled?

Reader, have you ever written yourself a letter?

Over the past few decades, our interactions have changed dramatically. In our fast-paced lives, consumed by tech, I often wonder if we've lost the true *art* of communication. Whatever happened to the postcard? The short note that reached your gran weeks after you'd returned from your break, regaling stories condensed into a tiny space, aimed at one person, the recipient, because you cared to share something just with them? The postcard only had space for a few passing thoughts, but the dominant one being the wish that the reader were there with you.

Even the greeting card has lost its sentiment. The process of carefully selecting a design, finding a biro in *that* drawer and scribbling furiously in the hope that it still works, then (physically) writing a personal dedication to somebody worthy of the time it took you to buy, write and post the card, is dying out for many. Instead, we see an automated four-step online process with a reminder sent to you on the same day, every year, and a questionable photo plastered on the front.

Do you remember when the text message used to consist of one long, considered paragraph instead of a flurry of one-liners? No little dots to indicate typing or seeing if someone was online, just one hit. Then we'd await the response (probably while playing Snake).

Whatever happened to the letter?

Recently, I went to Rhodes and for five indulgent days I allowed myself the pleasure of relaxing. To actually do the thing that we are meant to do on holiday, recharge and ignore the stresses and strains of the life that I had popped on pause. I read books, swam in the sea and drank watered-down cocktails with a smile plastered across my sunburnt face. I tried hard not to check work emails, muted news, entertainment and *Real Housewives of Another State* or *Selling Something*, and switched off. One afternoon when my phone was dead as I hadn't charged it (sorry, who was I?), I sat and people-watched. I observed a group of sunburnt Brits drop off into the water. I marvelled at a lady who was now reading her third book. And then I clocked a man. It wasn't his tiny solar-system swimming trunks that perplexed me (although you could clearly see

Uranus), but the fact that he was on a lounger, pen in hand, writing on a piece of paper. He seemed to be writing a letter. For the next hour and a half (three Long Island Iced Teas and two bowls of olives), I watched this unfamiliar scene unfold, all the while asking myself, when did I last write a letter?

Was it while I was at school?

I found English Literature class in senior school hard. You had to think about grammar, tone, reasoning and why things were portrayed in the way that they were. For me, it was a difficult, confusing, draining lesson. At the time, I hated reading. I hated 'old' stories on stormy heaths, or period pieces with dialogue written in a way that I'd never speak. There were characters that I didn't relate to, with stories nothing like mine. Nothing like the feelings brewing inside of me. Nowhere in the tomes of literature devoured and dissected did I see myself.

What I loved in those lessons, however, was my pencil case. It bulged and had far too much in it. A compass that pricked me every time I dived in. A protractor (I'm sorry, did I ever use that?). A ruler that folded in the middle, because of course you always need 30 centimetres to hand. And pens. I had black, blue, red, green, pink, even gel ones. An all-inclusive buffet of implements, my pencil case had it all. It made me happy. Sure, the majority of the pens were chewed at the end, an unfortunate by-product of nerves. When in doubt, or if I needed a moment of escape, I'd rummage. In a pencil case of comfort, looking for an answer to a question that I didn't even know I needed to ask. *Who am I?* I wish that I could go back in time and tell that little gay boy, my younger self, who was desperate to silence the comments and disappear into his pencil case, that it's going to be OK. You'll find the pen, the colour you need, the right tool that will help you. The thing that will make a hard day easier. Your tribe. Your letter in an alphabet not yet included in the school curriculum …

I slowly learned to love English Literature, not because I started to understand every story that I read, but because I discovered that sometimes, people out there were writing new ones, and fighting for mine. I learned to appreciate that when we can't articulate what we want to say, nothing can quite replace the written word. Sure, fast communication has its benefits, but I sometimes wonder if we had to wait days, weeks or months for a response to something we had written, would our words be more carefully considered? Would you share more and beat around the bush less? Would the anticipation allow for further excitement to build?

So, reader, we are going back to basics. Rediscovering the lost art of letter writing.

What follows is a collection of letters from our own fantastic rainbow of correspondence. A selection of incredible people who have generously gone back in time, dived into their pencil cases, opened up to their younger selves and described their important journeys. Some of the contributors are part of the LGBTQIA+ community, others are allies or friends who have written to a loved one. All are offering a helping hand to anybody who has experienced, or is currently going through the experience of 'growing up different' in our complicated society. I invite you to open these letters of vulnerability, love, anger, grief, laughter, pain and hope, knowing that whatever you have been through, or are going through, you are seen, understood and never alone.

We can't re-write our own pasts, but we can keep communicating in the hope that it will help the futures of others. Our collective hope is that the words that follow in this book give you comfort and strength, make you laugh or nod in recognition, and allow you to feel supported. Because everyone deserves a letter in a world where we are all just trying to find one that fits. There isn't a silent consonant, or one more important than the other.

Letters to My Younger Queer Self

These are our letters.

If you have never written a letter to yourself before, I also invite you to have a go. You never know, it might be just what you need to read.

Love,
Daniel

The fridge list our younger selves really needed:

- Exercise – but do it for you, not for anyone else.
- Come out when you're ready – but don't be forced into it.
- Smile – regardless of braces.
- Love – repeatedly.
- Wear a condom, go to the clinic, take the right tablets.
- Don't be an online troll. Or any sort of troll.
- Be kind – not many people are.
- Keep communicating – write a letter.

Daniel Harding

Author and Broadcaster
Gay
He/Him

Dear Younger Me,

I wish you could stop worrying. You are seventeen. *Please stop.* It makes me anxious to think of the panic attacks that lie ahead for you. The fear you are bottling up inside, the put-downs and name-calls that await you, the challenges you will face.

OK, let's move forward.

Daniel, I have some good and bad news. Here goes … I hate to break it to you, but you are thirty-seven years old and not married. *Breathe.* The good news, however, is that you can actually get married. Yay! It's not illegal – at least not for you living in the UK. (You could even do it in a church … If you wanted to. You don't. But rejoice in that fact.) And … *breathe.*

There's still hope that you will marry. I mean, you are currently on five separate dating apps and averaging around three dates a week. OK, four. You'll learn what dating apps are in a few years' time and you'll have a love/hate relationship with them. They will also use up a lot of your screen time – you'll learn about screen time soon, too. However, sixty-four countries across the globe still claim being queer to be illegal and it can even be met with the death penalty. And it's 2025. Yeah, we still have a pretty long way to go. Though, as people chant every June, who needs Pride, right?

Oh, and we're using the word 'queer' again. It's not an insult anymore. I know you won't understand that after the word was weaponised against you at school, beaten around your face and thrown at you like dirt ... But we've reclaimed it and it's kind of empowering.

Breathe.

Some things never change.

You do not like fish. No number of ex-boyfriends (you've had a few) attempting to make you try tuna or black cod because 'it's not that fishy' has altered this. You still hate anything from the sea or pond and have to defend this statement constantly. Ducks being included in this is still a struggle for some to see, but I'm with you, it's wrong. Wet bellies and beaks ... yuck!

Your anxiety around sex and STIs and infections has wavered, but it's still present. You have not got over this yet. However, an incredible new drug, PrEP (pre-exposure prophylaxis), is making this transition easier for you and millions of people, which prevents you catching HIV.

I'll let that statement soak in for a minute.

Back? OK, here's the bad part: you aren't on PrEP. Yes, I'm angry at us too. You are currently worried about the damage it could do to your kidneys. Yes, we still research on forums a lot, but now it's called 'googling'. (You'll learn about Google soon, and overuse it too.) You do want to start taking PrEP, not for the rubber-free sex, but for the peace of mind and extra barrier against HIV. We're working on it, though, getting closer. There's still a stigma attached to HIV/AIDS, but you're doing your part to break this. I'm proud of you. We still have much to learn and a long way to go. There is no known cure, yet.

Breathe.

You haven't had a nose job and you hate the lines around your eyes that have developed with age (stress and laughter), but you haven't had Botox … yet. You laugh a lot, though. Like, loads. And so perhaps those lines tell your story. But your book isn't finished, yet.

Your mum divorced him.

Breathe.

So, you will all be safe and OK in the end. Hang in there, I know you're finding these years incredibly hard. Unfortunately, it's going to get tougher before it gets easier, but you will be OK.

Letters to My Younger Queer Self

You will *all* be OK.

You're nearly eighteen and about to come out to the world. You hate the thought of it; sick to the stomach, you're crying a lot at night. Quietly. Alone. But your dad isn't going to disown you. I repeat, he isn't going to stop loving you, Daniel. It won't be easy, but believe me when I say this, you're actually going to be one of the lucky ones. Many will have a tougher battle ahead of them. Thrown out or abandoned.

Breathe.

You will not end your life. It won't end your life. You will become more comfortable in yourself.

Queer.

In fact, not long ago, before writing this, you went on national TV and spoke about being gay to millions of viewers on mainstream television. You are using your voice to help others (you hope) and I'm proud of you. You wrote a bloody book about it. (Fuck you, 11 Plus!)

You no longer hate yourself.

Breathe.

You are a work in progress. Love is a strong word, but you're getting there. You often wonder if that's why you're still single. Yes, you *are* still single. However, you've loved and been loved. You've had some great boyfriends and some questionable ones. You'll come to learn that being broken down or made to feel smaller than you are, will be a 'them' thing, and not your fault. Breaking free will never feel so good. The good ones will come, even if fleeting – in fact, you'll meet a man soon who will change your life. Enjoy it. I'm jealous of you going through that – I want to do it all over again. But you will love and learn. It's all valuable.

Stop looking back. Please look forward, it really does race by. Give that neck a break!

I want you to know that you're going to be a best man at least four times – I know that's surprising to you right now, especially when you're unsure if you have many friends. You were never the pick of the team, but now do Barry's Bootcamp like you belong in the army. I know sometimes after PE lessons, you wait until everyone's gone from the changing room and finally get dressed, wiping away tears, worrying about if you'll find anyone remotely like you. But my gosh, do you! You have incredible friends, boys and girls and thems (more on that soon) – who are now men and women and theys – and you have other people around you from the community that you love and are learning so much from. My gosh, there's lots to learn. My gosh, you say my gosh a lot. You've come a long way from the little chubby kid who used to lie to his parents about his friendships … You've grown, you've found them.

Breathe.

Make time to travel constantly – alone and with your best friend, Darren – because your adventures together will feature in books to come. You'll finish off each other's sentences and exchange looks about memories that you share. (Yes, you did sleep together, once – but you'll come to learn that a lot of friendships form this way in the community – and this was/is a special one.)

There are plenty of things that I don't want to tell you. You'll experience them, make mistakes and learn from these. But live in each moment, especially in New York when everyone else goes to bed and you get back up, change and head to a bar someone recommended to you. Please know that you are actually incredibly brave, Daniel. Yes, you still hate compliments but those times will hold great memories in the future.

You have a future.

Breathe.

Also, I have to tell you, you grew into your voice and you found your comfort but have a long road ahead. Sometimes an exhausting uphill struggle. Save energy for it. But please stop hating yourself. Learn to love. Embrace your gay.

Enjoy each moment because with every second you do, you are becoming the man you never thought you'd be able to be.

Be kind. Forgive. Love.

I love you.

Yours, Daniel x

Letters to My Younger Queer Self

P.S. *Barbie* was made into a mainstream movie and became the highest-grossing film of 2023. The world loves it. Those dolls have come a long way since you played with them secretly and cut their hair too short. Laura eventually forgave you for ruining them!

Alaska

Drag Queen and Singer
Gay
He/Him

Dear Younger Self,

   I have a serious problem with this assignment as I vehemently believe that travelling back in time and tampering with the past is a sure-fire way to throw off the current timeline. If you read this information from your future self, it will surely alter the course of events within your own life and beyond. Reading this letter could cause massive devastation, nuclear disaster, or worse – *The Golden Girls* might never get made. Perhaps there are some general, evergreen pieces of advice that might be useful to you and anyone reading this without throwing off the space-time continuum:

- Learn to meditate. Even if you don't do so regularly, knowing how to do it will give you something to do if you are ever buried alive.
- Stretching is good for you. Gluten is not.

- If you watch *Sex and the City*, watch it in the knowledge that Carrie Bradshaw is an unsympathetic protagonist – not a role model.

I want to avoid getting too specific with you, Younger Self. If I tell you that you'll grow up and be paid way too much money to dress up in long blonde hair, excessive make-up and tight, flowing dresses, I'm not sure if you'd believe me. I also doubt you'd believe that you drive an electrical space car and have a magical device in your pocket that can play any episode of any of your favourite TV shows on command. That's pretty cool though. I won't tell you, however, that this same magical device is also a source of pain, worry, annoyance and this new, ever-present thing from the future we call 'anxiety'.

If I attempt to tell you useful information that's good for your health, like 'don't drink too much', it could have the same effect that all those years in the D.A.R.E Program [Drug Abuse Resistance Education] had. In which case you'll end up not drinking or doing anything against the rules until you're eighteen, and then you'll do pretty much all of them all at once the second you get to college. Which I guess worked out fine. But as a general rule, avoiding cocaine and drinking a little bit less is pretty much categorically always better in every imaginable way.

If I tell you that you'll grow up and be paid way too much money to dress up in long blonde hair, excessive make-up and tight, flowing dresses, I'm not sure if you'd believe me.

I could tell you not to make really stupid decisions. Don't drive your bike home drunk without a helmet from Faultline. Don't drive out of the city to meet some guy and then get stoned and realise you don't want to hook up with him, so he makes you leave and you have to drive terrifyingly stoned all the way home.

Don't try to hitch-hike your way out of Burning Man to get back to LA. But wait – if you don't do that, then you'd never end up losing your job at Circus of Books, and then you'd never end up moving to Pittsburgh, and then you'd never end up getting into a relationship with Sharon, which would then mean you'd probably never get on *RuPaul's Drag Race*. And if you don't end up on *Drag Race*, I'm not sure what you'd be doing because being a Ru Girl has been the only job you've ever held for longer than a year. See, this timeline business is tricky.

I could tell you to appreciate your parents, especially your father, because you will be faced with losing him in a very sudden and terrible way. But then if I told you that, you'd probably see to it that he never gets on a motorcycle again and then you'd really be cramping his style and taking away a hobby that he truly loved. So just be nice to your parents and tell them you love them.

I could tell you to make really shrewd business decisions – like, creating a make-up line right after you win *All Stars*. But then you'd have as much money as

Trixie Mattel and honestly, no one needs that much money.

But no – enough! I want you to avoid reading any of this, Younger Self. Your drinking, drug use, career missteps and litany of all-around horrible decisions have created a rich and bizarre tapestry that led you to the place where you are now. You're almost forty, you're generally healthy and generally happy. You're on your patio, the sky is blue and there's a hummingbird sucking nectar from the feeder your sister got you last Christmas – and in this very moment, for you, everything's pretty OK.

But now that I think about it, the current state of the planet Earth is terrifying, abysmal and borderline hopeless. Maybe if you read this transmission from the future it will cause massive changes to your life's timeline and therefore to the world. Maybe there's a chance there will be less war and predation. Less dishonesty and greed. Less hunger and pain.

So, Younger Self, read on. What harm can it do?

Alaska

Lotte Jeffs

Author, Journalist and Parent
Queer
She/They

Dear Lotte,

    You're fourteen years old and you're in a German class at school (look, you'll be thankful for being able to pronounce *danke schön* when you blag your way into Berghain in your late twenties). You know the other kids in the class are passing around a note about you. They're laughing, whispering, calling you names and the teacher isn't stopping them – she's too worried about being popular to side with you and tell them off. You wonder if you should just walk out of the class, but you don't have the confidence. It'll take you a good fifteen years after this to give yourself permission to leave a situation that's making you miserable. I wish you hadn't been so good at letting things wash over you. You might not think bullying is affecting you, you might not ever want to feel like a victim, but a thick skin isn't always a good thing – although, granted, it helped you make it as a journalist!

Letters to My Younger Queer Self

Here's what I want you to know. Those girls and boys who took the piss out of you at school, called you a lez, pointed out your hairy arms, threw your workbooks out of the window, stole your stuff – they're not the ones interviewing the likes of Lady Gaga and Kristen Stewart for the cover of *ELLE* magazine. They haven't written four books or travelled the globe staying in five-star hotels (I know you've only been to France right now but hang tight because you marry a successful travel writer and the world becomes your oyster!). You don't know or care what happens to them because your life expands in such a beautiful, glamorous, exciting way, those bullies don't even make the footnotes of your story.

You're such an anxious child – telling your little Mexican worry dolls your fears each night, putting them in a box under your pillow, hoping they'll be gone by morning. But look, right now you've nothing more to worry about than nailing the 'Stop Right Now' routine so you can perform it with your best friend Will at G-A-Y when you start frequenting the Soho club in Sixth Form.

I'm sorry to say that some things you didn't even know you needed to worry about happen. Your parents split up once you finish university, your beloved older cousin dies of a brain tumour, Will gets very ill with cancer and that girl you meet when you're eighteen and she's thirty – yeah, bad news. Please split with her the first time she

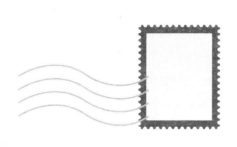

Those bullies don't even make the footnotes of your story.

calls you pathetic, the first time she gives you the 48-hour silent treatment, the first time she tries to convince you not to see your family. For God's sake, don't stay with her for eleven years!

The thing is, though – you can deal with all this stuff. It's sad and hard, of course, but you have amazing friends and you find within yourself a strength and positivity you never knew you had. Despite the bullying, you don't ever feel shame or confusion about being gay. News flash – you get your first girlfriend in Sixth Form and I'm pleased to say queerness remains a happy through line. It fills your world with funny and fabulous people, sends you to the best parties and on the most incredible adventures. Being gay is consistently a great part of your life, so you're right to be out and proud at sixteen. And you're definitely right – it's not a phase!

In your twenties it takes you a while to realise you're in a bad relationship and that pretty girls can be controlling and emotionally abusive too. But that same steely resilience that helped you survive school and zone out the bullies so you could focus on the few friends you did have and on working hard (yes, you're what we used to call a 'boffin' – own it, cos you get straight As and a First at university), it was the same spirit that meant you put up with this woman for the best part of your young adult life.

But don't despair. You meet your person before you're thirty. Jenny's the kindest, most loving, easy-going and supportive woman. She builds you back up after you eventually leave your toxic ex, and while you're grieving for your cousin Billie, who was devastatingly gone too soon.

Like something out of a fairy tale, Jenny helps make all your dreams come true. You get married and as you've always hoped, you have a baby! A little girl who you get to make up stories with, play Sylvanian Families with and share in silly jokes. Being a parent is the thing you are most proud of, more than any of your books or big jobs – taking care of her and helping her become a wonderfully kind and funny and creative person is your biggest ever achievement.

Oh, and guess what? There's a big surprise coming courtesy of your little cousin Romy, who has always been more of a sister to you. And it's not the fact she's queer too – that was pretty obvious from the age of eight. But this shy girl who loves Arsenal and won't ever put on her shoes when you ask her to becomes a famous pop star! I KNOW! Wild.

If I could ask you to do a few things now to help you in adulthood, it would be to worry less, smile more and stop being so good at ignoring bullies. Walk away from them sooner, and in the words of your little cousin's hit song, 'Enjoy Your Life'!

Love,
Lotte

James Longman

Chief international correspondent,
 ABC News
Gay
He/Him

Hi James,

    So, I've caught you at a pretty important time in your life. Once you get over the shock of receiving this letter from an older version of you, I'd like you to think about how HUGE it was for you to have just told your best friend that you're gay. It was no small thing. You're sixteen. You have horrible skin (don't worry, it will clear up), you had to tell her quietly at her kitchen table while her parents were in the next room, but right now, it means there is at least one person in the world who knows who you really are. So, I want to say: Congratulations! Be proud of yourself! (And by the way, she won't let you down. In fact, years from now you'll do the reading at her wedding and you'll go on foreign holidays together.)

    You don't have hindsight yet, so let me lay it out for you. Your dad died when you were a kid, you were raised

Being gay is going to make you a better person. You will learn empathy quicker than others.

in a relatively traditional if not conservative home, you're an only child and your relationship with your mum is not great (I know, it's spooky how much I know!). And hiding is hard, and lonely. You're at an all-boys, Catholic school and you don't feel you can tell anyone there. That's totally fine. You're feeling angry because hiding who you are is exhausting. You're worried people will find out. That a word, a movement, a look will give you away.

I can't change the past with this letter, but I can tell you that hiding in this way is only going to tire you out. And by the time you get to university and have only told a handful of people – and still not your mother – you're going to hit a mental health crisis. So please learn to give yourself a break. Don't be so hard on yourself. Everything you want is out there waiting for you. You are a lot more than your sexuality, but being gay is going to make you a better person. You will learn empathy quicker than others; your struggle will give you a strength that many around you won't have; you will build extraordinarily deep and long-lasting friendships with a lot of amazing people and you will be the example that others need.

And I know right now that the idea of telling someone else about being gay fills you with dread. You're thinking that telling just one person will do for now. And that's fine. But over time, you're going to hear other people's coming-out stories and you'll realise that your experience, however unique it may feel now, has been shared by millions through time. Some have had it worse, others have had it easier, but there's a community waiting for you with love and understanding. Without giving too much away, not only are you going to be able to tell more people, you'll eventually sit down and hear the coming-out story of the man you'll marry. And you'll stand up in front of all your friends and family and tell them how much you love each other. And you'll look back on this moment in your life and realise something very simple: It was that singular decision you just made to come out that made it all possible.

Congratulations on changing your life. You're just getting started.

Future James :)

P.S. Stop wearing that fleece.

Ella Morgan

TV Personality
Trans
She/Her

To Evan,

    I never thought in a million years that I would have the opportunity to write this, the same way I never thought that I'd be sat here today as the girl I've always known I am inside, Ella. But as they say, dreams do come true. One thing I want you to remember is that dreams can be reality. If you are strong enough to deal with the fight and the inner/outer battles, then you can accomplish anything.

    In life, everybody has struggles. Everybody is given a purpose, and your purpose is to be a voice for so many trans people, by being your true authentic self. Being unapologetically you and honest, real and relatable. You will help so many people along the way. So never give up. Always shine bright and never let anybody tell you that you're not good enough. So many people will be jealous that they don't have the guts, like you, to change your life

Mum and Dad and your brothers will absolutely adore you and stick by you. It's hard for them in the beginning, but appreciate them and be grateful because they are one in a million.

for your own happiness. There will be a lot of hate along the way, but always remember where you started and how far you've come.

Your story is different and colourful to the rest, and being trans and being Ella is your secret superpower. There will be times when you don't feel good enough and you feel that you shouldn't be deserving of being here, but please don't ever quit or end it, because the world wouldn't be the same without the little shining star that you are. Your family will struggle, but it's because they love you and worry about you. Give everybody time and patience to let you flourish. But never ever have any regrets, just learn from the mistakes you make, and boy, do you make a lot of those! Life's too short to live with regrets but still remain that kind soul who makes people laugh and smile and you'll be fine. Tell your family you love them as much as you can and appreciate their acceptance, because you may not get a chance to say it again. But also, don't forget to look in the mirror and tell yourself that you love *you*, because the demons can – and will – get the better of you, but you need to remain here and be present for so many little trans boys and girls, who you become a beacon of hope for.

Don't wear those terrible wigs in the beginning. Get some make-up lessons asap. But don't ever change that crazy loud personality. Wear less-skimpy clothes, please

– you will look like a hooker otherwise. Don't go hard on the Botox and fillers, also!

Don't let men treat you badly or walk all over you, cuz men are trash (well, not all of them!).

Don't sleep around, lol! You are enough, you've always been enough, and you will continue to be enough, but don't focus on anybody but yourself: you're number one. Please carry on with the journey to becoming Ella, because she's kind, beautiful, loud, loving, funny and individual. Mum and Dad and your brothers will absolutely adore you and stick by you. It's hard for them in the beginning, but appreciate them and be grateful because they are one in a million!

Learn to love yourself before you attempt to love yourself through other people's validation and acceptance. It will take time but it's so worth it in the end, and don't ever forget that.

You are incredible, Evan, and I'm so proud of you and everything you become and achieve. You're always with me and will be until the end. So, stick by me for this wild journey called life and we'll be together having the best time.

I love you x

Adam Theo

DJ and Musician
Gay
He/Him

Dear Adam,
    Subject: A Letter of Recommendation

    Ten Undeniable Queer Anthems

- 'Your Disco Needs You' – Kylie Minogue
- 'True Colors' – Cyndi Lauper
- 'You Make Me Feel (Mighty Real)' – Sylvester
- 'Vogue' – Madonna
- 'I Will Survive' – Gloria Gaynor
- 'I'm Coming Out' – Diana Ross
- 'Relax' – Frankie Goes To Hollywood
- 'Freedom' – George Michael
- 'Y.M.C.A.' – Village People
- 'Dancing on My Own' – Robyn

Five Songs That WILL Make Us Dance

- 'Something New' – Girls Aloud
- 'Love at First Sight' – Kylie Minogue
- 'Man! I Feel Like A Woman!' – Shania Twain
- 'Commander' – Kelly Rowland
- 'Push the Button' – Sugababes

Sincerely,
Adam

Nadia Whittome

Member of Parliament
Queer/Bi
She/Her

Dear Nadia,

You're eleven years old. You're doing 'am I gay?' quizzes on Mum's laptop (and then clearing the search history because you're worried about anyone thinking you're gay). You're relieved when the result is 'not gay' (but you wonder if you answered the questions entirely truthfully). Definitely 100 per cent straight.

It will take you another few years to come to terms with the fact that you are, in fact, attracted to women. You'll come out to Mum while watching *Ackley Bridge*, because in Nasreen Paracha you can point to another brown, queer girl and say, 'That's what I am', without having to explain anything else. A few weeks later, you'll attend your first – out – Notts Pride in Hockley. The drag queens will be incredible and it will be way more fun than going as a 13-year-old 'ally' to Pride on the Forest Rec with your friends, for some reason collecting free condoms and keyrings (neither of which you have any use for) from all the voluntary sector stalls.

A few years later, you'll come out again, this time in the public eye, as an MP. As LGBTQIA+ people, we're continually coming out, in every new situation, to every new person in our lives. In some ways it's a bit easier when you're a public figure because if you're out, most people already know.

I wish I could tell you that life will be plain sailing. It won't be. You'll continue to face challenges. Some of your fears might materialise, but that's fine. Even though you're still a kid, you've already weathered storms. You'll weather some more. Whenever you feel like the world is ending, it won't. Whenever you feel like you can't take any more, you will. You'll learn that you're stronger than you think. You'll grow into an adult who takes care of herself, you'll meet someone you love completely and who loves you too, and you'll have a supportive community around you (it includes your school friends, who will remain some of your closest friends, and that's precious).

You'll have to navigate the compounding systems of oppression that come with being queer and a person of colour at the same time – both from outside and within those communities. You'll sometimes feel excluded from the solidarity that exists in both spaces and the racism and homophobia that can occur in each community respectively are particularly painful. But you will also find pockets of hope and joy. Spaces and projects that are both queer and People of Colour-led will be particularly dear to you: from UK Black Pride to magazines like *Gaysians*, *Burnt Roti* and the sorely missed *gal-dem* to club nights like Pxssy Palace, the queer Bollywood night Hungama or the incredible South Asian DJ collective Daytimers (their remix of *Bole Chudiyan* is fire). You'll read *Burning My Roti*, Sharan Dhaliwal's book about navigating life as a queer South Asian woman. You'll feel seen and wish you could somehow go back in time and give it to your younger self.

You'll also have to reconcile your queerness with your Catholic upbringing. You only go to church on high days and holy days but – having been baptised by your uncle, who's a priest, and raised by your mum, who grew up in a convent – Catholicism was always a strong presence. You feel hurt knowing that, when your parish priest talks about sin, he means you, and you internalise this homophobia without even realising. But later in life, you'll become friends with Maria Exall, the first out lesbian President of the TUC, as well as a practising Catholic with a PhD in theology (and a total legend). You'll share her (socialist!) address on St Oscar Romero in the family WhatsApp group. Through other LGBTQIA+

Kiss boys. Kiss girls. Cherish your friends, because they're the people who will stand by your side through the ups and downs of life.

people in your life, particularly older ones, you'll learn about 'chosen family' as well as blood family – both are very dear.

I've mentioned already that you'll become an MP – weird, isn't it? It's certainly not what you imagined for yourself. Even though you'll start following the news and having opinions – a whole lot of them – at a young age, for a long time you'll see politics as something that's done to you and your community: by much older, white men in suits, talking from the TV screen about crackdowns, cutbacks and tough decisions. Through joining your teachers on picket lines and helping to organise your first protest, you'll learn that politics isn't just what is done to you: it is also how you respond, all the things you can do to force them to listen.

You will be elected – firstly as the Labour candidate, and then as the MP – against a backdrop of a pretty vicious (albeit tiny) local campaign against LGBTQIA+-inclusive relationships and sex education. In the years that follow, homophobia and, especially, transphobia in politics will get much, much worse. Standing for office, you won't expect LGBTQIA+ rights to become one of the main issues you're associated with, but you will have to speak out. You'll watch senior Tories crack jokes about what's in trans people's pants, while millions of people are forced to skip meals to pay their energy bills. You'll hear politicians spend more time worrying about children asking to change their name and pronouns than record-breaking numbers growing up in poverty. Many of the attack lines used against trans people will echo insults and tropes used against gay people in the decades before you were born. You'll learn that progress isn't linear and that our hard-won rights can never be taken for granted.

You've always been a private person. You've already learned to keep your pain inside, to put on a brave face and say you're fine when you're not. You don't like gossip, don't like people knowing more than they need to – your life is none of their business.

You'll still be protective of your privacy in your adulthood, which can be tricky when you're a public figure. You'll make the difficult decision to open up about having PTSD. It will feel uncomfortable, broadcasting to hundreds of thousands of people a struggle that only a handful of people in your life previously knew about. You'll wish it wasn't necessary but you'll be glad that, in a small way, your honesty might be able to help people who are fighting similar battles.

Living with trauma can feel lonely, confusing, overwhelming – doubly so when you're young and queer. Sometimes, lying awake at night, you'll find yourself wondering if bad things have happened because you're queer, but I promise it's not.

You'll see your identity weaponised. It will be hurtful and infuriating to see people who claim to care about survivors portray as predatory the communities you're part of. You'll hear racists smear all people of colour as potential abusers, with no regard for Black and brown victims. You'll see the far right and transphobic 'feminists' spread similar tropes about the LGBTQIA+ community, not recognising or not caring that this makes queer, trans and questioning kids even more vulnerable and less able to ask for help. That's why it's so important for support services to be loudly and proudly LGBTQIA+-inclusive. Like Imara: a Nottingham charity supporting young abuse survivors, which has progress Pride flags visibly displayed from every window. Little gestures like this send a signal to queer and trans people that they can feel safe.

Unlike many MPs, you'll grow up relying on state institutions. You'll experience the impact of ever-growing NHS queues, school cuts and closure of local facilities. You'll feel the consequences of benefit cuts and see the way in which the Department for Work and Pensions (DWP) treats disabled people. You'll be failed by the police and social services, like they've failed many other women, people of colour, working-class people. You'll learn that, without wealth and privilege, you'll have to fight extra hard for the bare minimum and demanding your basic rights will often feel like banging your head against the wall.

Then you'll enter Parliament, and everything will change overnight. For the first time in your life, you'll have disposable income. People will be speaking to you differently, suddenly showing respect when they see 'MP' next to your name. You'll be surrounded by people brought up in a completely different world, who have a collection of holiday homes and admit to not having any working-class friends (I'm looking at you, Rishi). You'll be glad to be able to use your position to support constituents dealing with similar frustrations to the ones you had, speaking to them from a place of understanding and solidarity. There's an inherent power imbalance between working-class people and the institutions they're dealing with, including MPs. The power you have must be used carefully and redistributed as much as possible.

You'll be proud: not to be walking the corridors of Westminster, but to be able to amplify the movements that developed your politics, which gave you the rights you enjoy and made you who you are. You'll meet your heroes. You'll realise that the biggest among them aren't the people who give barnstorming speeches, but those working every day to make the world a bit more liveable. The cleaner who finds the time and energy after an exhausting shift to go to a union meeting and help organise a strike. The school kid who defies authority and walks out of class to demand climate action. Trans people who refuse to be silenced, despite the daily barrage of abuse they face. Queer activists stopping deportations. Sex workers building support networks to protect each other and fight for their rights.

As you can see from this letter, weird things will happen in your life and even stranger things will happen to the country. And I haven't even touched on the wildest bits yet. Government politicians spreading outlandish stories about children identifying as cats. Self-described progressives celebrating a guidance that would make schools hostile places for trans and non-binary kids. Amidst all the horrors, there will also be a prime minister who gets beaten by a lettuce ... But most of the news won't be funny at all, it will be frankly pretty terrifying.

You'll stand on the shoulders of giants: like the people who fought against Section 28 and ensured that you could hear about queer people at school and find LGBTQIA+ books in the local library. Learn from them, because decades later, you'll be fighting for another generation of queer kids, growing up in an atmosphere of hostility. But for now, enjoy being young. Don't feel like you need to have everything figured out – that will take decades, or perhaps your entire life. Take it day by day. Remember that every experience is a learning opportunity. Kiss boys. Kiss girls. Cherish your friends, because they're the people who will stand by your side through the ups and downs of life.

And maybe do that quiz again, this time without lying. I'll tell you a secret: you're not the only queer kid in your school, or even in your friendship group. There are people you know taking the same quizzes and asking themselves the very same questions right now – let them know they're safe with you.

Nadia

Paul Davies

LGBTQIA+ Disability Activist and former
  Mr Gay Universe
Gay
He/Him

Dear Me,

I know you're hurting in ways you never thought possible. I know how it feels to lose so many people you love, in such a short space of time. To see your world torn apart and thrown upside down, feeling like pieces of you have been taken with them.

You hide away and isolate. You've tried to numb the pain, to quiet the storm in your mind, and now there's shame and guilt that you continually put upon yourself by comparing yourself to others.

No matter how hard you push it down, it keeps finding its way back, doesn't it?

I recognise those sleepless, tired eyes and that welcome smile you frantically put on to hopefully fool others … After all, it's not fair to put on anyone else, is it? *Is it, Paul?* You question a lot now too, don't you? What you are, who you are, why you are and where you are – just as the path started opening up it felt so clear. Newfound friends, family, work, a community ... But now, in this endless mist of grief and loss you see no rainbows. Just storms. You wonder if you're even worthy of being a voice, of standing for others when you're struggling just to stand for yourself.

Well, I'm here to remind you of something: all of this hurt, all of this pain, doesn't define you. Yes, you've been through hell and it's left scars, but those scars are living proof of everything you've survived. They're proof that you're still here, even when you thought you couldn't be. You're stronger than you know, even if you can't see it right now. You can, you will, and you shall! You have the people of Wales, your queer family, your disabled community, YOUR HUMAN RACE ... You can't do it alone, don't do it alone. Be brave and reach out! You're a 1984 baby, after all – you're strong! This isn't where your story ends, this is only the end of Act One of three ... something to give you motivation to come back!

Look, boyo, the world still needs your voice, your compassion, your resilience and that Rhondda Valley's cheeky mess and Redcoat smile! You have the power to turn all this hurt into something meaningful. Look at how you were born – ten fingers are clearly overrated! So, take it one day at a time, one breath at a time. Allow yourself to heal at your own pace, without judgement. You're more than the grief, more than the loss, more than the self-doubt, more than labels – you are being human. Real. One day, you'll look back and realise that rainbows are truly in every cloud and that this was the chapter that showed you just how powerful you really are.

Until then, be patient with yourself. You're worth it.
NEVER STOP BEING YOU!

Cariad enfawr (lots of love)
Ti (you)

Radam Ridwan

Transdisciplinary Artist
Non-binary
They/Them

Dear Radam,

There's a video of you in the depths of the internet. You were selected to be the lead, Danny Zuko, in a Year 2 *Grease* play. I'm pretty sure it was because you were the cutest kid with the darkest mop of hair in the class rather than pertaining to any semblance of performing talent. You couldn't actually dance to save your life. And in a production where prodigal kid gymnasts were literally cartwheeling from side to side, you struggled to woo poor Sandra Dee with a meagre shimmy. You did have a certain camp pizzazz, though. You couldn't keep a straight face. You broke character to look at the side of the stage, where your father was holding a video camera, watching you watch him.

I watch that clip of you every now and then on rainy, introspective days. I stare at you and see a face of freedom. A body filled to the brim with profound, uninhibited joy. A version of you before children had begun to inhabit the prejudices of their parents. A version of you without constraint. Sure, *Grease* is an excessively heteronormative film – and to be honest, you're much more of a 'Rizzo' – but something about the way your limbs move through space like strawberry jelly is utterly transfixing.

I just want you to know, you taught me how to live in the moment. Because of you, I know that profound, uninhibited joy can't only be found in youth. It can be captured again and again and again. So, that's exactly what I do. I dance like everybody's watching – and I still don't give a fuck.

There's an image of you held in my mind.

Before your sisters were preoccupied with boy-filled cars roaring around corners, they dressed you up 'like a girl'. They simply wanted another sister, but unfortunately for them, your parents had brought home you. They waited until the house was empty and raided the closet for your mum's fancy cosmetics. One painted emerald green on your eyelids, while the other finished your look with a bright red lip.

You pursed your lips as a mirror was held up to your face. You were stunning, a damsel-in-distress with pointy cat-eyes and Elizabeth Taylor lashes. That didn't stop the tears from streaming, the green flowing into the black and the white diluting the creamy circles of red. In the mirror, you saw someone yet to be conceived, but that made Them even more alluring. Their image stayed with you always. A painful reminder of who you weren't allowed to be, and who was meant to be.

You were too young to understand that this was a turning point. As you ran to the bathroom, rubbing away all that beauty, pushing down all those feelings, you wondered: 'What if I was another sister – would that be so bad?'

I just want you to know, you taught me how to dream. Because of you, I know there's more to us than who we are thought to be from the outside. That I don't exist merely in the imagination of others. So, although the world doesn't allow us time to get to know ourselves, I am worth every single second.

There's a photo of you on your parents' bedside table. You're wearing a basketball uniform that's a little too small for your waist, holding up a medal that's a little too big for your shoulders. Your parents adore this picture, they say, of their 'little boy'. That day you won the under-16 boys' state basketball tournament. Unlike the *Grease* play, you had performed, earning Most Valuable Player. Your father gave you a high five, the highest form of flattery from a Southeast Asian parent. Your sisters sat on the sidelines, cheering on their MVP 'brother'.

The photo shows you smiling. Inside, you are melting. You were a winner, but your teammates had scrutinised the limpness of your wrists, the inflections at the end of your sentences, the softness of your spirit. What had changed?

A body roll like Jessica Alba became 'don't move like a girl', blonde tips in your hair became shouts of fag, a simple earring became a fist to the face, a party dress became the death of people who look just like you. And you started to despise the things that put you under the heat of the spotlight. Retreating to your room as you arrived back home, throwing your bigger-than-average-for-your-age shoes back in the closet. The world told you to stand in line and you had no choice but to hide for the moment.

I just want you to know, you taught me how to survive. Because of you, I know that to love myself, even in private – is powerful. That I know my mind, body and heart better than anyone else ever could. So, sometimes I disguise in plain sight, saving myself for me – I don't owe the world my entire being.

There's a portrait of you in the pages of *Vogue Italia*. You appear harder, more fully formed, cheekbones painted for the gods. The stunning damsel-in-distress with Elizabeth Taylor lashes you had envisioned in the mirror all those years ago. As the camera snapped, you are focused on serving – the world was but a secondary character to your brilliance. But as you stomped home in 6-inch heels, focused on surviving – your self-built shelter faded away. Someone stops in the street to laugh and film, another stops you in your tracks to shout and intimidate.

The comments say you've 'glown up' but that doesn't stop them threatening to strip away your shine. They say it gets better when you come out, but you still need to re-introduce yourself every time you step out. You say you are proud of those photos, but they don't show all that you are.

You called your mother in tears just to hear a familiar voice. She had seen the portrait of you on Instagram and asks if you prefer 'handsome' or 'beautiful'. You replied, 'Whichever, as long as it refers to the person I am in this moment, not the version of me that's in your head … although, "gorgeous" is nice.'

You wonder if she will ever see you as you. If you can chip away at the image of you that appears on the bedside table. Your mum paused over the phone, finally declaring, 'Well, I just wanted to say you look gorgeous right now.'

I just want you to know that you taught me how to reinvent. Because of you, I know that I am a work in progress, never needing to be finished. That beauty is not born, it is grown – not in your skin, but your words. That

They say you've come a long way since you were younger, but that's not true. The only difference between you and I is that now you have the space, tools and paint to exist as yourself in this world, the way you always wanted.

you are more than your trauma. So, I will recreate myself as often as I desire. I don't exist for their attention.

There's a letter I'm trying to write to you. Glitter-painted fingernails are tapping the laptop, pondering what I can say to you. I'm supposed to give you the SparkNotes from the 'glow up' version of you, advice from an enlightened figure, but all I can think is – what can I tell you that you didn't teach me?

They say you've come a long way since you were younger, but that's not true. The only difference between you and I is that now you have the space, tools and paint to exist as yourself in this world, the way you always wanted.

You are the person in the YouTube video, the person in the image held in your mind, the person in the photo on your parents' bedside table and the person in the portrait in the pages of *Vogue Italia*. And each is as strong and authentic as the other.

I'd be lying if I said I didn't wonder who you would've become if you'd been allowed to breathe. If your face wasn't pored over for signs of faggotry. Your body wasn't stripped of all gestures of femininity. Your spirit wasn't squashed into a tiny little box. But that doesn't do you justice. You withstood all the bullshit – and came out the other end just as beautiful, inside and out. No matter how many ways they tried to tell me you're gone, or that you shouldn't have existed in the first place, you stuck around.

I just want you to know that you taught me everything I know. Because of you, I know that I am all that I need. That I can't be captured by a single image, or a slanted opinion. That we are the things that we stand for, not the things that bring us to our knees. So, I will dedicate this letter to you.

I owe you the world.

Love,

Radam

Anonymous
A Reminder for Our Queer Best Friend

To my darling Queer Best Friend,

If only you knew.

Let's face it. School was a bit shit. It was bloody hard. Kids have zero respect for each other and you have to work hard to fit (and stay) in with the crowd. Girls can be such little bitches: 'You don't have Kickers?'; 'You eat Tesco own-brand crisps?'; 'You shower at night and not in the morning?'; 'You haven't got your period yet?'. Boys can be vile arseholes (chewing gum in the hair – that bloody happened and Mum had to cut it out. She then chased that poor boy down the road! Embarrassing).

Corridors were like an assault course as soon as that bell rang. The Year 7s lugging enormous Kappa bags and the lanky Year 10s carrying nothing but a pen (maybe a few cigarettes too), bashing into the Year 7s like they're bowling pins.

The girls' toilets were awful. Thick smog from the powder foundation choked the air like what I imagine the backstage of *RuPaul's Drag Race* to look like. Not to mention the absolute stink of cheap cigarettes – how the

If only you knew the magic and (literal) sparkle you brought to others' experiences.

F did the teachers not know that people were smoking in those loos?

One week you'd be in the circle of trust with your 'friends' and the next you'd be out. Sometimes all your 'friends' would be going to the party and you'd not be invited because one girl didn't like you (again, true story). It was pretty brutal and anxiety-inducing. No wonder such a high proportion of millennials suffer with their mental health. We've been through it.

If only you knew, though, how much you genuinely softened all the edges of that shit for EVERYONE.

If only you knew the magic and (literal) sparkle you brought to others' experiences at school. I do have pictures with you adorning glitter (but I'll keep those to myself).

If only you knew how much humour and laughter you created with such ease. Drama class would have been nothing without you. You had more creative energy in your little finger than anyone in that school. You could take the most depressing of plays and turn the whole thing into the most entertaining piece. You absolutely drove the (once Thespian) drama teacher mad with your continuous, hilarious interruptions. It was because of you that her slowly delivered 'would you just shut up' phrase became infamous. She definitely hated you, we all bloody loved you!

If only you knew then how popular you would be. Ask anyone ... Everyone remembers you from school and for good reasons. You weren't an attention-seeker. You weren't out looking for that spotlight, it just found you. You are naturally funny, warm and magnetic. You could talk to anyone, find a common level with all teenagers and approach any crowd. Some crowds at school were so intimidating and, let's face it, downright scary, but you could hold a conversation with anyone with such ease. That's a life skill that most people never get close to. It's also a life skill that will see you catapult in your career – you just get people.

If only you knew how much you'd tease out the gay tendencies of the bullies. So controversial, but it still shocks me today to find out who 'approached' you during our school years to 'experiment'. Some of the toughest bullies (downright shitbags to you in younger years) and the popular, utterly gorgeous guys saw you as the guy who was leading the way and obviously knew what he was doing. They (many of them!) wanted a bit of that! And why wouldn't they? You're hot. Can you even believe that you had an entire 'affair' with a straight (to be clear, single) guy for months, who still to this day is 'straight'? Even better, you secretly snogged his best mate too! This sounds highly critical and I don't mean to make light of the internal battle he and others were going through with their sexuality. The point here is that they saw you as someone they trusted with that complexity in their emotions and confusion around their sexuality: you were the person who they could turn to.

As a younger you, could you have imagined the impact you would have on them?

If only you knew what a trailblazer you were too. You were one of only two or three boys at school who was openly gay: that's not representative of the statistics at all, nor (I imagine) is it representative of what the diversity looks like in schools today. I wonder how many people in younger years would reference you as someone that inspired them? It will be more than you'd imagine. You did something brave in being that person unashamed (I'd say unafraid, but I don't want to assume you weren't afraid) of being who you are.

It's people like you who change the world, one small suburban Essex seaside school at a time.

You won't realise the impact you had. You won't accept praise for this because you're modest and you did it for you.

I hope you now know that what you did for you has rippled all over and that your story carries through into so many of our lives. You are magnificent and I remain inspired and astonished by you every day.

If only you knew then.

L x

Cody Daigle-Orians

Creator of Ace Dad Advice
Asexual
He/Him

Dear Cody,

In our first year of studying theatre in college our acting professor asks us what we want to do when we graduate. We say, 'I want to be a playwright.' Our professor smiles and says, 'That's great. You're the only person who can write your chapter in the Big Story, right?' He is right, and so far, we're doing a good job of writing our chapter. It's got lots of surprises that I won't spoil for you. But I can say, when you get to where I am now – age forty-eight – you're nothing and everything you hoped we'd be. Here's some advice to help you write our chapter, a few things to hold on to when you feel like we've lost the plot or when you wonder if it might be easier for us to just stop writing it.

You're going to spend a long time thinking that you're not enough. You'll compare yourself to others and see only what you think they have more of: more beauty,

Your queerness is not your enemy. It's not a liability. It's not a brokenness. It's actually the most powerful tool you've got. Your queerness will transform you as many times as you'll allow it.

more smarts, more courage, more sexual prowess, more masculinity, more talent, more value. Sometimes, you're right. Other people do have more of those things. But you already have all of the things you need to make a positive mark on the world. You have them in abundance. Those things feel like liabilities – your sensitivity, your softness, your caution, your over-analytical brain, your role as an outsider, your uncertainty and (most of all) your queerness – but these are the parts of you that will shape your future. These are the parts of you that become your power. Do your best to tend the garden they're growing in, even if you're unsure what they're growing into.

Tell the truth. Care deeply about the truth. Look for the truth in everything you do, in everything you feel, in everything you encounter. Look for the truth in other people. Look for the truth in everything around you. And even when you think you've found the truth, ask more questions to find the truth beneath it. That pursuit – that searching – is the real work of your life. Take it seriously. The truth liberates you.

The world is not going to be particularly kind to you, but you're not alone in that. The world isn't particularly kind to many of us. People will reject you, leave you, shame you and diminish you when you show yourself to them and to the world. So, your instinct will be to retreat from the world. Resist that. Sure, it feels a little safer and you might avoid some hurt, but it doesn't make you (or anyone else) happier. As much as I would like to spare you the pain of our journey, I recognise the pain is what makes us who we are. It hurts, but we survive it. It sucks, but we learn from it. The only things I regret from my 48-year-old perspective are the things we didn't attempt because we were scared of what the attempt might feel like. All the times we tried, all the things we worked through, all the moments when we faced hard things bravely – these are all points of pride.

Try to remember that the only appropriate answer to the people who will be hateful to and about you is being more of yourself and making more of what you're good at making. Meet the unkindness and bigotry of the world with equal and opposite care for the world. Have a sense of humour about it. But also, have a sense of your responsibility. Learn as you teach. Think of your journey through the world as the work of making space for others, not making a space for yourself. Be present and grateful for every opportunity to exercise your gifts and repair the world a little.

Final thing, because I want you to enjoy this journey as much as you can: your queerness is not your enemy. It's not a liability. It's not a brokenness. It's actually the most powerful tool you've got. Your queerness will transform

Letters to My Younger Queer Self

you as many times as you'll allow it. The more you embrace it, the more you'll see possibilities in the world that others don't see. The more you lean into it, the more you'll feel at home in your body. The more you live your queerness openly and proudly, the more you'll find other people like you, other people who are also changing the world for the better. Your queerness is you. If you abandon it, turn away from it, hide it or reject it, you lose yourself. And that's not the path we're meant to take.

Good luck. Stay strong. And don't give up. It's worth it for you to get to where I am, so we can see who we can continue to become.

C

Philip Baldwin

HIV Activist
Gay
He/Him

Dear 16-year-old Philip,

Hello, Handsome!

This is you in twenty-four years' time. Well done for surviving your horrendous teenage years. Introverted, lonely, frightened and bullied by most of your classmates, I think about you often and especially how you helped me to be the person I am today.

It is your resilience, work ethic and bravery, having the vision and sheer self-belief to see beyond those school gates, that will get you through. You are special. I wish I could breathe life into your downtrodden soul.

I want to tell you that your life is going to change dramatically. There might be surprises along the way and your priorities are going to change, but there will be huge achievements which you never thought possible. A warning, though – not everything will be ideal as you go on your journey of self-discovery.

Letters to My Younger Queer Self

At sixteen, you will lose your virginity. It's 2001. You'll be in a gay bar in Glasgow on a Friday night. You'll go back to a guy's apartment. Unfortunately – but typically – I can't remember his name. Brown hair, perhaps – early twenties? He was handsome and the sex was good. Admittedly, you're drunk and have nothing to compare it with. On the one hand, I'm pleased that for once you were having fun. Go, Philip! But with hindsight, it would be nice for your first time to be with someone special.

Section 28[1] has just been repealed. Its malign presence means you know next to nothing about gay relationships. The newspapers write that gay men behave a certain way. Drink. Sex. Repeat. Only make sure it's somebody different each time. Do not use this as your template for the next two years. Instead, text some of those nice young men back for a second date.

A few months later you will come out to your one friend at school. She will say the right things and won't blab about your sexual orientation. When you're seventeen, after clubbing in Glasgow, a guy's going to try

---

1 Section 28 refers to a part of the Local Government Act 1988, stating that local authorities in England, Scotland and Wales 'shall not intentionally promote homosexuality or publish material with the intention of promoting homosexuality' or 'promote the teaching of the acceptability of homosexuality as a pretended family relationship'.

Everything is going to change. No longer furtive about your sexuality, almost overnight you'll go from socially awkward to gregarious.

to rape you in a hotel room. You'll escape him. Sadly, telling people would have meant outing yourself to your school and parents, which you aren't ready for – not yet. Don't feel guilty for not reporting this to the police. You were the victim. Furthermore, you have just received your acceptance letter from Oxford. Is it any surprise you don't want to jeopardise everything?

Oxford is going to be all you dreamed it would be. Everything is going to change. No longer furtive about your sexuality, almost overnight you'll go from socially awkward to gregarious. You will have the confidence and ease you've picked up from dating people much older than you on the gay scene. I'm looking forward to you having friends and some of these friendships will be lifelong.

It's going to be several years after you finish your degrees that you become fully aware of the changes that have been taking place since the turn of the millennium around LGBTQIA+ rights. The equalisation of the age of consent was legislated for in 2000 and came into force in January 2001. You turned sixteen four months later, in May 2001. You're enjoying the new freedoms available to you. You take much of it for granted, though. With the glow of Labour's 1997 election victory, maybe you think progress is inevitable?

Why not get involved in campaigning for social justice? After all, it's what your life is going to ultimately revolve around! Attend a protest or two, seeing as you'll be doing lots of that in the future? What about the wider world and the impact you can have?

After university, you'll go into the City to work as a lawyer in financial services. Six months after beginning at the law firm, aged twenty-four, you will be diagnosed with HIV and hepatitis C. That's right. Six months after starting the job of your dreams, your life will become a nightmare.

You don't need to maintain the façade that you're the out and proud gay man who has it all. Just reach out, access some peer support, talk to your friends. It will save you lots of nights crying alone on your bathroom floor.

It will be three years before you fully come to terms with your HIV diagnosis. Telling your employer and parents will be liberating, like coming out again. You will learn that there are effective treatments for HIV. That means you can't pass the virus on and can also expect a normal lifespan. It is the stigma associated with HIV that will impact you more. That stigma will make love and some friendships more complicated, maybe cause you to even lose some. But did you want those people in your life anyway?

There will be high points even as you come to terms with your HIV. In 2011, you will go on secondment to the law firm's New York office. You will work incredibly hard, but in other ways, you'll be having the time of your life. You'll love New York and the USA. Savour every moment. Do not cancel your trip in July 2011 to Chicago because you are exhausted. You will have neither the time nor the money to do trips like that when you're a writer and human rights activist. And please accept one of those many invites to Fire Island, which you turn down because you're working late in the office until midnight. You will never be twenty-six again.

Warning! There's a big surprise, even bigger than the HIV, coming. Please ensure you are sitting down as you read this. At the end of 2012, the major turning point in your life will happen. You will begin to attend Christian church services. I know, right? Sounds absurd, but I promise this is true. Don't be cross with me, laugh or be embarrassed. It's an understatement to say that you will have a deep and meaningful relationship with faith.

You're going to fall in love with Jesus.

Eventually you might even think Christianity is cool. As well as religion, you have magazine columns, write opinion pieces for the papers, have a radio show and do a little TV, commentating on current affairs and occasionally presenting – although none of it will pay you much.

The writing and campaigning begin in 2014, initially around HIV and hepatitis C, but this soon expands to cover asylum, homelessness, international human rights abuses and faith inclusion. You leave the job as a lawyer to do this full time in 2015. You are privileged to have the voice that you do and also, as a writer, to be introspective and vulnerable and to share that with a wider audience.

It's when you're thirty, in 2015, that you will be confirmed at Southwark Cathedral, which houses the UK's only HIV/AIDS chapel. This will be a beautiful moment, combining two aspects of your identity.

In 2021, you will be elected to represent the Diocese of London on the Church of England's General Synod, its legislature. At sixteen, you're at best a complacent agnostic, if not an atheist, so you may not know this, but the General Synod is the only body apart from the Houses of Parliament which makes laws for England, because the Church of England is the Established Church. You are one of two General Synod members living openly with HIV.

Being gay, living with HIV and a being senior Anglican will make you outspoken and determined to make a difference, but also controversial. You're going to play a key role in the Church becoming more LGBTQIA+ inclusive. It will be OK, though, because your faith is intertwined with your human rights activism. You're on the right side of history. You will be empowered by your own lived experience of discrimination and stigma. And, ultimately, you were elected to speak truth to power.

Some final reflections are that there is nothing wrong with being ambitious, but do not be surprised if the course that life takes is completely unexpected. It's the many mistakes as well as the successes that will make you who you are.

The HIV was a curveball, which you will adapt to well, and you will lead an emotionally and intellectually much more rewarding life, where through your writing, activism and platform on the General Synod, you are able to influence national and international policy. And occasionally, directly positively transform another individual's life. Is that not one of Jesus's key messages from the cross? That each life is uniquely precious, that it's possible to see His face reflected in all his creation and that makes every personal struggle worthwhile?

So, remember that your time will come, stay hopeful for the future and continue to dream.

Love and solidarity!
Philip
xxxxxxxxxxx

Shivani Dave

Career Queer
Non-binary
They/Them/Theirs

Reminder – Don't Rush

Hey pal,

    I know you're probably not feeling too great, but you should know that one day you will start to feel like your lungs are full of air. You'll be able to breathe in deep and feel a sense of calm one day. You'll find your truth and nothing will feel as freeing. You'll be working on making sure other people get that same feeling of salvation and liberation. Don't be mistaken: you won't have all the answers, you will probably have more, and more, and even more questions. But the anxiety deep within, causing you turmoil about who you are or why you are here, all starts to become clear. When you learn that you are not alone, that you have community, friends and family who see you for how you longed to be seen. They hear you and celebrate you for all your idiosyncrasies.

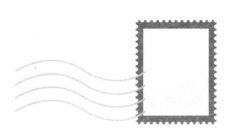

Find the places where you feel at home, where you feel at ease. Let your guard down and trust that those who are important in your life won't leave.

What makes you different isn't a weakness, you'll be asked to speak in front of those classes you were once kicked out of for being 'too loud', 'too challenging'. You see, one day people won't say you're questioning authority, they will see the glee that radiates out of you from within, they will say you're living authentically.

All those 'debates' at the dinner table should have been a sign you're a fighter. You're working tirelessly for other people and that's beautiful. Don't forget to take time for yourself, look after your mental health. And I mean that. Not just the buzzwords and the bougie yoga retreats. Find the places where you feel at home, where you feel at ease. Let your guard down and trust that those who are important in your life won't leave. Because they won't, not the ones who matter. Not the ones who will watch you age and celebrate your hair as it starts to turn grey.

Because you make it to that stage, something you never thought you would see. Feeling at peace, you have the privilege of growing older. No longer feeling like a fish out of water. With language and learning and this community, finally, you realise you were never a fish but a shark that needs the ocean to breathe.

It all makes sense, why you coloured outside the lines. You were never meant to be boxed in because that box may as well have been your coffin. Believe me when I say, there is so much more you have to live and explore. So,

Letters to My Younger Queer Self

do me a favour: don't rush to get to your final days, live out each one until you see the bright brilliance of the light inside you that is still to come.

    Love yourself always,
Shiv

Anonymous
A Thank You to My First Love

Dear First Love,

As I sit down to write this letter to you, I am filled with a sense of reflection and gratitude for the journey we shared together. Meeting you at a young age and exploring love together was both exhilarating and challenging. We were both figuring out who we were and what we wanted from life, all while trying to navigate the complexities of our relationship.

Our connection has journeyed through various stages to this point, but the memories we created and the lessons we learned continue to shape my perspective to this day. Since our time together, I embarked on a journey of self-discovery and personal growth that has led me to where I am today. I learned so much about myself, about love, and about navigating the complexities of being in a gay relationship.

One of the most significant lessons I learned is the importance of authenticity and self-acceptance. Our relationship taught me that it is OK to be true to myself, coming out and navigating the intricacies of being a gay man, particularly one who may not fit into society and its narrow definitions of masculinity. As a gay man who may have been perceived as 'straight acting', I understand the challenges of coming out and the pressure to conform with ideals. It requires courage, resilience and a willingness to defy stereotypes. I learned that true strength lies in embracing our unique identities and refusing to conform to societal norms that seek to confine us.

Our journey together also taught me to embrace vulnerability, communicate openly and prioritise mutual respect and understanding. These lessons have not only enriched my personal growth but have also shaped the way I approach relationships and connections with others, both in my career and at home.

As I look back on our time together, I am grateful for the role you played in my life and the ways in which you helped me grow. Our journey may have had its challenges, but it was also filled with laughter, love and shared experiences that I will always cherish.

As we continue on our individual journeys, I hope you know that I carry with me fond memories of our time together. I wish you nothing but happiness, fulfilment and love in all that you do. May you always stay true to yourself and embrace the unique person you are.

Thank you for being a part of my story. Here's to the friendship we shared and the growth we experienced together, and as we grow older (yes, we are growing older – hopefully, you have accepted this now!), our friendship continues to mature.

Continue to be you, first love that helped the rest, unapologetically authentic you.

xx

Christine Diaz and Kirstie Pike

Content Creators and Co-founders of
  @onairplanemode__
Lesbian
She/Her

Dear Younger Christine and Kirstie,

 As we write this letter to you, we can hardly contain our excitement for the journey that lies ahead of you. On a serendipitous day on a rooftop in New York City, you will meet and begin a story that intertwines love and all your dreams in the most beautiful ways. Little did you know that this moment would lead to over seven years of partnership, both in life and in business, filled with joy, challenges and profound growth.

 Christine, growing up in a very conservative and religious family, you often feel the weight of your heritage and the expectations that came with it. Your father's Mexican traditions and your mother's Chinese and Peruvian cultures, each with their own reservations about the LGBTQIA+ community, make you question whether you could ever live your truth openly and proudly. Remember that it's OK not to have all the answers. Life is a series of discoveries and each challenge you face is an opportunity to learn and grow. As a first-generation American, I know you hold fear that you will never be accepted, constantly wondering what your life would be like and where it would take you, but I urge you to keep believing in yourself because life will be more beautiful than you can ever imagine.

Kirstie, you will find that your upbringing in the South, surrounded by its own set of challenges, has only made you stronger. The lessons you will learn about different people and perspectives will prepare you for the incredible future ahead. Don't worry, every difficulty you face now will shape you into the resilient and compassionate person you become.

To both of you: keep taking chances and taking risks. The moments of internal struggle, the nights of questioning and the fear of coming out will soon fade and you will live your truth ... so much so that you create a career out of it. Built off your love and authenticity, you will share your personal experiences with people all over the world that being out and proud is possible and that having unconditional love is possible. Together, you will become content creators who travel the world, sharing

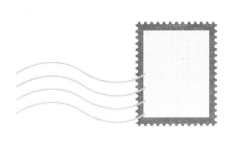

I urge you to keep believing in yourself because life will be more beautiful than you can ever imagine.

your experiences, knowledge and creativity with an online community that will be inspired to live their authentic truths.

Christine, everything you manifested in your youth will come true and even more so. You will meet the love of your life in Kirstie and you will explore the world together, experiencing incredible adventures that will change you forever. You will connect with amazing people and work with brands you once only dreamed of. Trust your instincts and know that everything will be OK. Your journey is just beginning, filled with incredible opportunities and experiences.

Be kind to yourself, you will see how you have and continue to make your parents proud soon. Despite your initial fears, your family will support you and even embrace Kirstie as part of the family. You will succeed in everything you do. Take that leap of faith and remember that the corporate world is not the be-all and end-all. You will find your true passion and work in a field that fills your heart with joy. Through your content and meaningful conversations, you will bring positivity into people's lives. All your dreams of making a positive change are coming and currently happening, and you will continue to rise above challenges. You will fill the gap of visibility for queer representation in media. Embrace peace and happiness, knowing that you are making a difference.

Letters to My Younger Queer Self

Kirstie, you will find that your creative side becomes a path for those seeking representation. You and Christine will become a source of inspiration for others, especially for young queer women in love who didn't have the role models you needed growing up. As a duo, you will teach people how to travel safely, explore the wonders of the world and work with government officials to make positive changes and support the LGBTQIA+ community. Your impact will be profound, touching the lives of many around you. Never doubt how amazing and talented you are. Your success will be nothing short of extraordinary, making waves in places that need it most. You will attract incredible energy and your life will be filled with friends and family who support you unwaveringly.

As you both continue to grow and learn, you will become powerful leaders in your advocacy and activism for human and social rights, not only for the LGBTQIA+ community but beyond. Your dedication and passion will inspire and create lasting change and your journey will be a testament to your strength and brilliance. You will have the girl of your dreams, your twin flame, by your side. You will become speakers, educators and travel experts, creating a safe space for people like you, a space you didn't have before. Watching you both grow and accomplish incredible things will be a joy.

Remember to continue manifesting and believing in the power of your dreams. The sky's the limit, so dream big. Everything you aspire to achieve is within your reach if you believe in yourselves and your vision. Manifest your desires with confidence and watch as the universe aligns to bring your dreams to fruition. Your journey is guided by your intentions and the limitless potential within you.

We can't wait for you to see all that you will achieve. Manifest. Keep your heart open, your mind curious and stay true to your values. You are loved and supported and the best is yet to come.

With all our love,
Christine and Kirstie

Anonymous
Letter to My Bisexual Brother

Dear T,

'That's so gay', 'don't be gay', 'gaylord', 'you're gay', 'your mum's gay', 'that's bent', 'doyoulickadickaday' ...

All playground torments that were very normal to use at the ripe age of six or seven, back in the early 2000s. It was such a common insult back then. Everyone at school used it. I remember calling you 'gay' when you were annoying me and you certainly returned the insult right back to me. No one truly understood what it meant. Not at that age anyway.

Being your older sister, what really got to me is when the notorious playground bully, who shares the same first name as you, started calling you gay. Again, without probably knowing its definition, but I hated that he was being mean to you. No wonder it's so hard for men who lived through this playground cruelness to come out as gay or bisexual or trans or non-binary. It was literally hammered into us that 'gay' was a bad thing. Something to be ashamed of. Absolutely sickening and I can't believe it was such a recent turn of events.

It's easy to say if I could turn back time, I'd tell you to ignore them. Being gay isn't a bad thing. Why is this even an insult?! Kids in the 2000s were brutal and it's shocking that the language they were using so flippantly had such a damaging impact on young men and women growing up. Thankfully, these terms being used as an insult is dying out, hopefully making it easier for younger people to open up to their loved ones more freely without worrying. That said, I recently came across someone who used it in frustration. I called him out on it. He came back and said, 'But a lesbian told me it was OK, she found it funny.' Obviously societal changes haven't got through to him yet. Poor boy.

I don't know when you started to think you were interested in men, but I can only hope you weren't bottling it up for too long. You probably were, though, and I blame it on every time you heard it used in a negative way (including by myself). I think we both know that the way I found out was less than ideal – for you, for me and for the other person involved. But I did always know this would be a funny story to tell in the future. I hope you agree.

When I found out, I'm not going to lie, I was worried for you.

You know I always want the best for you and I just want you to settle down with someone because I know

Letters to My Younger Queer Self

that's what you want. The reason I was worried was because I thought it was going to be a lot harder to find someone. Small pool of potential dates, especially in a relatively small city. You'll be pleased to know I'm not worried about this anymore.

Thank God for online dating.

I guess all I want you to know is that everyone is so proud of you – Mum, Dad, me and I know that Grandma would have been as well. I'm writing to you anonymously because I know that you aren't fully there yet – you aren't 'out' to everyone – and that's OK. Whatever you decide is OK. I am here every step of the way.

The world is your oyster. You can do anything that you want. I'm excited for you – we all are.

From, C x

Alysse Dalessandro

Digital Creator
Queer
She/Her

Hey girl,

 Thank you for being here; for taking time for you. You haven't always made yourself a priority, but that's not your fault. You were sold a lie that love meant putting others first at your own expense. I'm so proud of you for all the work you've done to see that true love starts from within. You didn't love yourself for a long time. Mostly because you didn't know you could. You've been through some difficult things. I'm sorry you had to experience that pain and that trauma at such a young age. I hope you stop beating yourself up for what you've been through: you were a kid and you were just trying to survive.

 I'm sorry that you felt like you had to hide or shrink yourself in order for others to notice you. I love you just the way you are and I don't want you to hide anymore. You're kind of a badass and all of the things you've been

I want you to know that you're smart enough, pretty enough, well enough, good enough, queer enough. You're enough.

through don't make you less than others. They have made you tough as hell; you don't give up.

I hope you can learn to trust other people. I know you've been hurt by those people who should have protected your heart, but don't let other people's mistakes stop you from allowing caring, empathetic, good people in. You're independent and that's great, but that doesn't mean you have to do everything alone. It's OK to need people sometimes, and most importantly, you deserve that! Believing that good people exist isn't setting you up for failure. In fact, I think that belief that you're worth people caring about is the first step in letting those good people in. Will you still hurt? Will you still cry? Sure, but you'll do so knowing it's not because you're 'the worst'.

I hope you destroy that thought process forever.

I know you're letting go of the anger that has masked the sadness you've felt for a long time. I know it's not going to be easy, but feel that pain, feel that discomfort. It's real, but it's not going to break you. Allow yourself to feel those feelings so you can see that you're OK, because you're OK and you're going to be OK.

I want you to know that you're smart enough, pretty enough, well enough, good enough, queer enough. You're enough.

Letters to My Younger Queer Self

Destroy the idea that how you feel about yourself has anything to do with anyone else. You decide to be free, and I know you can do it. Don't settle for anyone who makes you feel like who you are isn't enough. You've got this!

I love you!

Alysse

Bright Light Bright Light

Musician
Gay
He/Him

Dear Rod,

Checklist to My Younger Self:

- Music is your safe space, now and always. Ace of Base was a GREAT first album purchase.
- But you should also learn scales. They're boring and so frustrating, but you're gonna need them (unlike trigonometry, which you somehow worked harder at).
- Be kind, be patient.
- Being the only boy to go as a witch on Hallowe'en in primary school was really weird – well done!
- You will learn to love your voice when you eventually find it.

Letters to My Younger Queer Self

- You have less time than you think with some of your favourite friends, so see them more.
- Your worst heartbreak will create your most life-changing song.
- And the boys you thought broke your heart in your late teens didn't, they kick-started it.
- Go to New York earlier in life.
- Put less pressure on yourself about romantic relationships. You – and they – are much better when you let go of that stress.
- People who initially are ashamed of you will eventually be very proud.
- Learn that everyone is battling something and the way they treat you is likely a cause of that, not because of who or what you are.
- You can, and do, make things happen without support. Never stop.
- Egg Everything bagel is the superior bagel flavour – have a few more years knowing that.
- The times you think you're boring, or other people act like you're boring, only make the surprise that you're not more effective.
- You should have bought those extra Tori Amos LPs on sale in FOPP for £5. They're £200 now!
- Spend as much time with cats as possible.

Letters to My Younger Queer Self

- Always be thoughtful, but don't second-guess yourself as much.
- Have more fun.

From,
Rod

Cyrill Ibrahim

Concert Pianist
Gay
He/Him

Dear Cyrill,

    The advice I would give to my younger self, older self and current self is to never lose sight of the bigger picture.

    It's easy to get caught up in worrying about what others think of us, but what really matters is what we want to express in our lives and how we want to live. A fulfilling life is one that leaves a legacy and is open to building towards that goal. For me, that goal is in the search for beauty, which I find in the quality of sound and in expressing myself truthfully. In the past, I have been too focused on success and other people's perceptions of me, but the moments when I was most truthful to myself were the most fulfilling.

    Currently, I see that the feeling I had when I was younger, I should have followed perhaps a bit more, which is to be purpose-driven rather than achievement-driven. Those two things are very different. Achievement is somehow subjective, superficial and not really satisfying, whereas the purpose that I feel I should have followed when I was younger, I'm more and more convinced, is the one that is most satisfying.

In my journey, I have always felt that I didn't belong to the world that I am currently in. I felt the bigger picture made me very much part of that. The confidence in the creation of the sound feeds through to the confidence I have been searching for in myself. I have had to understand the doubts which come with there being a place in the world for me and that I deserve to be here and express myself. Those doubts have often come from a place of self-doubt. Now I realise that doubts and the process to overcome this have led to gaining a better insight into myself and consequently made me stronger, mentally and physically.

Playing the piano is, in part, a physical undertaking. The pulse in music is the most fundamental aspect of music making. It holds the piece together, and in an orchestra, it keeps all musicians aligned. It is the framework that makes music make sense. It is the heartbeat to which we all contribute and tapping into the universal pulse gives us a sense of belonging. Doubts that have arisen from an isolated mind have prevented me

Be purpose-driven rather than achievement-driven.

from connecting to that pulse that unites like-minded people and the music I have dedicated my life to.

Despite my current doubts, I am now more open to tapping into this pulse and trusting that I am – and we all are – never alone.

Very best
Cx

Ben Pechey

Author and Presenter
Non-binary
They/Them

Dear Ben,

    I cannot remember the last time I sat down to write a letter. A letter is a personal thing, one that you write with an intended reader in mind. There is privacy in a letter that is rarely afforded to us. It is an intimate act to be treasured. A letter, in my opinion, should be truthful. So, I am entering into the unspoken contract with you, my younger self, of honesty. As I settled to compose this letter to you, jotting down my thoughts, speaking aloud how I felt, figuring out what I wanted to say to you, my first instinct was to tell you not to bother with this life. To give up, to roll over, to concede, to just submit to the pressures of being yourself. This seems like a very bleak place to begin a letter to you – younger me – as you are just beginning this life we get to share.

    Perhaps I should explain myself.

You see, I came to this sad conclusion initially because although you and I, or we, have consistently shown up, in every situation, exactly as we are, the problems we have encountered have always been at the hands of other people. For good reasons or bad, other people decided to make it abundantly clear that we don't belong, that we don't conform to the standards they place on us, that it is too difficult for them to fully understand who we are. Thus, they find it easier to shun, mock, malign, erode us until we simply no longer resemble the person we are.

There is a loneliness that has followed us, for as long as I can remember, that has been caused by the othering of those around us. It has felt as though no one wanted to claim allegiance to us, so we became a solitary nation, an island in a sea of confusion. A sad fact of life is that outsiders are always persecuted. Whether it is religion, shape, race, height, accent, gender or age, the human race has – and always will – find a way of ostracising differences. This was the modus operandi for how we have been treated. There was never a space for us to be accepted as ourselves, instead, the space offered to us required us to bend and change. The hole left in the puzzle was the wrong shape, so we had to change ourselves to fit, to survive.

A chameleon is capable of colour-shifting camouflage. Its skin becomes a mirror of its surroundings. In some ways, we adopt a similar pattern, mirroring the people who surround us, to protect us from predatory behaviour. These predators took aim at facets of our personality, so we decided to go within ourselves to protect other parts of who we are, were or will be. That camouflage hid the real Ben and projected what was easiest to cope with in the world. In many ways, it cost us so much. It meant that we didn't have as much time with innocence. We didn't have the time to get to know who we were in peace – we were too busy trying to figure out where we could fit in in the world. We may not have grown up the way we did if we were simply given the space we needed.

As time wears on, we leave domestic settings and head into a world that requires yet more camouflage. Except we finally know ourselves better. Only now do we have the confidence to be ourselves, to be Ben, unfiltered. Yet somehow, the world is still not ready, it has found new ways to be uncomfortable around us. We have done so much work, and been through so much, and yet we still fail in the eyes of society. The goalposts have been moved so many times that we don't know what we're aiming for anymore. You see now why I said that perhaps we ought not to bother. It has been exhausting, but it would be wrong for me to advise you not to try because the fact is, we are still here. We make it. Throughout all the pain of

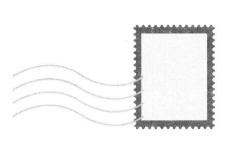

Life is painful for those who weren't built to conform. But society is to blame, not us.

being alive, of the bullies, of being misunderstood, miserable and feeling like the squarest of pegs in the roundest of holes, we are still here. That I am writing this letter is irrefutable proof that you, that I, that we, make it.

I am sad and it would be remiss of me not to warn you that growing up will be a painful thing for us. The hand we were dealt, for good or for bad, will cause us pain. People will remark that our choices will make our lives harder. That is not true. We did not choose this life. Life is painful for those who weren't built to conform. But society is to blame, not us. This is something I wish I had been told a long time ago and it seems that it is my job to do it for myself, so I am telling you now. I also want you to know that pain doesn't erase pleasure, it simply hides it from you. It may feel like there is so much life where we spend our time simply coasting, existing for the sake of existing. But there is so much pleasure and joy in this life and you will find it! It will wash over us some days. We will swim in deep moments of joy. We will be delighted by life. It makes being here worthwhile, that is our truth.

I'm not sure you've been told this, but we have a strength in ourselves. It is resilience. Resilience is not always understood. It's not a constant ability to rebuff tribulations, it's not unshakeable. Think of yourself as a houseplant – I'm picturing our Christmas Cactus: Lynda La Plante – which will wilt when left un-watered for too long. However, when tended to, having all its needs met, that plant bounces back verdantly, going on to bloom a month later. That is resilience, to weather the storm, even if it affects you deeply, but to come out the other side of it ready to try and bloom.

And weather the storm you have. Yes, we have scars from the past, the storm changed the way we feel. However, the fact that we managed to survive the tempest is something to celebrate. It hasn't been easy, but we still tried. Somehow, we have believed in ourselves. That belief has led us to help others and show other people that they can be themselves unapologetically. To give the gift of authenticity. We do that every day. Using what you have been through doesn't erase what happened – we can't change our past – but we share it to hopefully lighten the load of other people. We share it to stop other people suffering in the ways we did.

Hope for a better existence has brought you to where you are, Ben, and you are all the better because of it. My honest advice to you is do not give up on hope. It is the belief that things will improve. It is an optimistic outlook. It is the opposite of the pessimism I opened this letter with. I can't promise that every day will feel hopeful. However, if we hold hope in our heart, and have it in the back of our mind, we will see small things every day that make being here worth it.

Hope will be there for us whenever we need it. As a consequence, we know for a fact that the world is better because we are here. We live in it. We survive in it. We love in it. We are loved in it, unconditionally.

Believe in us. We make it worth it.

Love,
Ben

Calum McSwiggan

Author and Content Creator
Gay
He/Him

Dear Calum,

Right now, I'm thirty-three and writing to you from my apartment in London. The place is a mess because it's been a busy few weeks and I've been putting off writing this letter because I didn't know where to start. If you're receiving this as I intended, it's your fifteenth birthday and you're sat in your bedroom, absolutely terrified of the world.

You're going to be given a game for your birthday – World of Warcraft – and what you don't realise is that this game is about to change your whole world. At first, you'll play it because you think it's better than going outside, better than facing the reality that you're different, but with time, it'll help you to understand who you really are.

You'll choose a female elf when you come to choose your character. She'll be pretty and feminine and you'll tell yourself that's why you're choosing her. Because you'd love to date someone like her, right? It makes sense for a teenage boy to pick her. And that's what you'll tell anyone if they should ask.

But I know better than that, because I know that deep down, you have a secret.

I know these words are going to make you want to screw this letter up into a ball, to tear it into a thousand pieces, to set fire to it and do everything you can to ensure that absolutely nobody else reads it. But you don't need to worry, because there will come a time when you'll feel confident and safe enough to share that secret with the world.

I know you'll choose that female elf because deep down, you feel you resonate with her. Not because you feel you're a girl – though you will go through a period of questioning this – but rather, because you aspire to be someone like her. Someone who uses their femininity to feel powerful, someone who could have any guy she wants – because that *is* what you want, right?

I know you have a crush on your best friend. And I know that it's killing you. He won't ever reciprocate and he will swing for you when you finally tell him that you're gay. That black eye will feel like the most painful thing you'll ever experience, but it'll be the last time anyone ever reacts that way. 'I'm gay' will start to feel normal and people will respond with nothing but enthusiasm and warmth. That goes for your parents, too – don't worry about the fact they laughed at that homophobic joke on the TV. In a few years' time, all their friends will be gay and you'll question how you ever thought they wouldn't accept you.

One day you'll proudly hold your boyfriend's hand while walking down the busiest street in the country. You won't be nervous or frightened because it'll just be some ordinary Tuesday and it'll feel like the most natural thing in the world. You'll have forgotten that holding hands used to be considered some big rebellious act and you'll actually just enjoy the sensation of his hand in yours, knowing that you are loved.

One day you'll switch out that all-black wardrobe that you're hiding behind. You'll feel confident in colour and won't worry about how that makes you look. You'll even wear a t-shirt that says GAY AND PROUD in giant garish letters. You'll be on your way to your first Pride parade and you won't realise it then, but this will be the first of dozens of Prides you'll attend all over the world. You'll dance under rainbows and confetti in Australia, Mexico, Sweden and the USA – just to name a few – and as you travel the world, you'll feel not just proud in your identity, but grateful too. You'll realise that this is not some horrible curse that's been thrust upon you, but rather a gift that you feel so lucky to have received.

I know these words are going to make you want to screw this letter up into a ball, to tear it into a thousand pieces, to set fire to it and do everything you can to ensure that absolutely nobody else reads it. But you don't need to worry.

One day you'll go to the cinema and you'll cry because it's the first time you see a teenage love story that revolves around two boys. It's the thing you feel you missed out on more than anything, but it will have such a profound impact on you that you'll go home and pick up your laptop and start writing queer love stories of your own. It'll be hard work, of course, but you'll find a brand-new sense of purpose in living vicariously through your characters. You'll write the exact same love stories you wish you were experiencing right now – and although nothing will ever make up for what you missed out on, others will find joy in reading your stories and that will make it all seem worth it.

You'll one day work as a teacher and when your kids ask about your engagement ring, you'll tell them about the wonderful man that gave it to you. That engagement won't work out – you won't walk down the aisle (not just yet anyway) – but proudly wearing that ring will make an impact bigger than you could ever know. One of your students will later tell you that he likes boys. You'll be the first person he ever tells.

One day, you'll sit in your apartment in London and you'll open up that game you were given on your fifteenth birthday. Except this time, you won't be alone, because your best friend will be sat right next to you. She chose a female elf when she was a teenager too – not because she was gay, but because she was transgender. You both found yourselves through playing this game and although your identities are very different, you realise you're one and the same.

It'll feel like a full circle moment and suddenly, finally, everything will make sense. You'll realise that you're part of this incredible global community and that there are millions of people who feel exactly the same as you. You're going to spend your life meeting those people and the thing that nobody is telling you is that they're the best people in the world.

Being LGBTQIA+ is the greatest gift you've ever been given. I know right now it's hard and it's scary, but I promise the hard part is almost over: you're about to get everything you deserve.

Calum

Anonymous
Becoming Your Ally

I remember the times that we used to write letters to each other. There is one which is really special. You'd made me a ring binder for a birthday card (ever the creative) and I think it could have been one of the first times you'd given out your autograph! More of those moments to come – can you believe?!

This one read:

Boy meets girl, girl meets boy! They become friends, they talk! Boy tells girl he is gay! Girl still loves boy, boy loves girl! They have a strong bond. Friends forever!

And here we still are.

Times seemed to be alright back then, but I've learned so much since and realise that it was far from easy for you, growing up as a queer. It saddens me to know the struggles you went through, that you felt alone and couldn't speak up. You were always the life and soul, singing to us like a jukebox in the playground, making us choose a finger to see what song would come out. I had no idea of your internal struggles.

My advice ... Speak up. Express yourself.

The world has evolved, and although I realise it is still evolving for your community, I'd like to think there are more allies now. I'm still here. I still remember a horrible time in Zante. The onslaught of verbal abuse you received one night was uncomfortable to witness. But allies are like a bull to a red flag – find your bulls.

I'm glad you found your tribe eventually. Through them I've enjoyed many nights out and got an insight into your new world. Witnessed you grow.

My advice ... Find your people. Be brave and be bold. Try and accept yourself earlier. Find those that see you. And most importantly, be kind to yourself.

Looking back, I wish I could have been more informed about the LGBTQIA+ community, terminology, experiences and history so that I could be a better ally. Allies aren't saviours, but we need educating so we can be a good support network. You know I will always be there for you. I'm still learning too.

My advice ... Teach those that don't understand: your truth is powerful.

I hope my honesty and insight helps whoever reads this, should they need it, so they don't have as much of a struggle as you did.

Letters to My Younger Queer Self

Love always, to the one who keeps my memories alive from way back when. Your friend. Your ally. Your A.

My advice ... Find yours.

xxx

Michael Perry

Horticulturalist and Author –
 @mr_plantgeek
Gay
He/Him

I am a gardener and have loved plants since I was young (wayyy before it become trendy!), but the thing is, I used to be ashamed of it. At school they would call me a 'pansy' or a 'geek', so I kept my passion a secret from all my school friends. However, it was all OK as hiding among my plants gave me comfort and they became my friends. It was my own little safe world.

Of course, one reason I didn't want to share my passion was that it might expose my brewing sexuality. I was starting to think about boys, thoughts I was ashamed of, and another reason to hide away. Imagine, though, if when I was young I came across a wheelbarrow full of plants. A gift for me. The gift of a range of plants that would symbolise the strengths I'd need to be myself as I grew older. Plants that would grow with me over the years as I grew too. So, instead of a traditional letter, young lad, I am offering myself a wheelbarrow full of plants and hope:

- Buddleja – the Butterfly Bush – for courage. I'd love to remind my teenage self that I just needed to believe in myself more, to have courage. What better plant to symbolise this than one that overcomes all the odds, the humble yet resilient Buddleja!
- Senecio Angel Wings – for comfort and a warm hug. Sometimes you just need love and support, a simple warm hug. It's amazing what power that can have. This soft-touch Senecio would give just the comfort my younger self needed at the time.
- Cactus – yes, things might be spiky. I'd love to remind my teenage self that times won't always be easy, but you'll get through the other side. A prickly cactus symbolises this and, after all, those spikes are only there for self-protection and to help it to stay resilient …
- Dahlias – for flamboyance. It's OK to be you! I'd love to remind myself of that. When I was young, I was desperately trying to wear the same as everyone else. I didn't want to stand out, didn't want to wear anything remotely flamboyant. But, heck, dahlias don't care – they are dripping with colour and exuberance.

Letters to My Younger Queer Self

- Orchids – to symbolise sexual urges. I was so ashamed of my feelings that it wasn't until I was late into my twenties that I really blossomed into enjoying myself sexually. Orchids aren't shy, they symbolise honest sexual energy, and I'd love to have felt inspired by that when I was younger.

Anita Wigl'it

Drag Artist
Gay
He/Him

Dear Nick,

    Getting the opportunity to write to you today is nothing short of a delight. Firstly, you will be happy to hear that we haven't changed very much at all! You grow up to be the same smiley, happy person – full of joy and always the first person to make people laugh. Luckily, you grow out of all the terrible haircuts that you give yourself; you get the dog you always wanted (two, in fact!), you get married (and divorced, but I'll leave this one as a surprise) and you work as a full-time performing artist – all of the things you ever dreamed about. However, I didn't want to use this wonderful opportunity to connect with my younger self just to tell you what you are going to achieve, I wanted to help you. You see, life has been full of ups and downs (don't worry, though, you always have – and always will – continue to focus on the ups), but as you get older, you realise that the word 'downs' could be replaced with the word 'learnings'. I want to use this rare opportunity to teach you about my two most important learnings and what I wish I knew when I was your age.

Learning One – Sex, Sex, Sex!
In the beginning God created Man and Woman ... then a lot of other stuff happened and someone thought that creation and sex became the same thing. Fast forward to you now and you're a bit confused about the Birds and the Bees – or the Birds and the Birds, Bees and the Bees, whatever it is!

You have grown up in a Catholic household, where you were taught that sex before marriage is a sin and that sex is either an act of love or a little act to create a baby. This will blow your mind, but these points of view that align to the Catholic Church's views are only one idea when it comes to sex and you will discover that not everyone shares these views. Now of course sex can be special, but it doesn't always have to be, and learning this now it will save you a lot of heartache. (This heartache leads you to listen to sad Barbra Streisand songs on repeat, which, let's face it, isn't really good for anyone!)

The reason why I'm telling you this now is to prepare you for when you do have sex for the first time. You will think that by having sex it must have meant something to the other person, but it doesn't. This creates all sorts of confusing emotions for you and I want to set a few things straight – I wish someone had told me these things at your age to save me from anguish:

- Sex can mean something, but it doesn't have to.
- Not everyone has the same emotions associated with sex.
- Sex is meant to be fun, wonderful, explorative and not shameful.

Just relax and go with the flow of life. Also, on a side note, don't settle for anyone. You deserve someone who is at your level, so don't lower your standards just because you're lonely.

Explore, be patient, enjoy.

Learning Two – Main Character Energy
I have some good news for you – your life is going to be rather fabulous! You will get to reach your goals as a musician, transition your career into becoming a full-time drag queen, be on TV, travel the world with your own comedy show and meet the most amazing people. You will experience success, become absorbed in your career and put the character that you created, the good-time-gal Anita Wigl'it, at the top of your priority list.

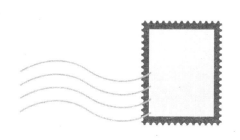

One of the best things that you will ever hear is, 'I am the main character in my life'. I'm so excited for you to learn this and to carry this main-character energy into everything that you do.

As amazing as Anita's success, is though, there is something that I need to encourage you to see. Even though she is popular, fun, silly and kind, she was created by YOU and based on YOU.

You too are a success, even if you don't always believe it.

You have a want and a need to prove yourself. I think after a lot of reflection I now know where this comes from. For most of your life you had to unfairly deal with, for want of a better term, being 'shat on'. People take advantage of you for being nice and easy-going, they are mean to you about your appearance, your mannerisms, etc. Due to these reasons, you have always thought, 'I'll show these people', and you do. WOW, do you do this! You go after your goals with a passion that I don't think I've seen in another person. You chase, you appreciate, but you are always looking for the next thing. This pushes your career to heights that even surprise yourself. However, I need to tell you that there is something more important than your career, and that is you.

Unfortunately, you will go through a dark time (remember the divorce I alluded to? Surprise!), but trust me when I tell you it's such a good thing for you. Obviously, there is sadness and you do reach rock bottom, but from this lowly position you are able to rebuild your life and put yourself at the centre of it. But you have worked so hard creating a life for Anita that you forgot to create a life for yourself. One of the best things that you will ever hear is, 'I am the main character in my life'. I'm so excited for you to learn this and to carry this main-character energy into everything that you do.

This message is very important for anyone reading this letter.

If you are a drag performer yourself, a lawyer, a doctor, a server, or whatever your role – just remember that you are more than what you do. In a world where we put so much emphasis on trying to be the best, trying to appear successful, it's important to let who you are shine and not be forgotten.

So, all in all, Nick, I'm excited for you! You are on this wild, incredible and joyous journey that we call life. There are good times and learnings, but everything you go through will shape you to become the person that you are today. I love you very much, and even though you want to, don't shave your hair. Trust me, from experience, it doesn't suit you.

All my love,
Nick

Alastair James

Journalist
Gay
He/Him

Hey Al,

How are you? You're scared, I know. You're sat on the edge of your bed, psyching yourself up to come out to Mum and Dad. I know, I've been there. It's been nine years since I was in your shoes (quite literally) and I hope by writing this to you, it gives you some comfort and reassurance in regards to what you're about to do.

I know what you're thinking – I always planned to come out when I had a steady job and was living independently, so in the worst-case scenario I'd be able to survive. And yet here you are, not sure where you're going in life and back with your parents after university. Not exactly living the dream. It's OK to feel scared. I did. But believe me, doing this now is absolutely the right thing to do. It will quite literally change everything for you, and writing to you now, as a 31-year-old out and proud journalist working for the LGBTQIA+ publication

Letters to My Younger Queer Self

Attitude, I can tell you it will make everything better for you.

And starting from now, the places you'll go, in every sense, the people you'll meet, the things you'll do and the steps you'll take are truly beyond anything you can imagine. The person you're about to start becoming really is the best version of yourself. I can't say I'm 100 per cent there yet, even now, but we're both on the way. And it's all because you're about to take that first, very big and very brave step.

However, in the spirit of honesty, it won't always be easy. But this will bring you and the family closer together. That feeling of forever holding your breath is about to ease. Like most people, they're about to meet the real you for the first time, every wonderful, messy and awkward facet. You've spent such a long time pretending to be someone else, someone acceptable, that you've prevented everyone seeing who you really are. I remember sitting across from Mum at the dinner table and seeing a look in her eyes that told me she knew I was in pain. Now, that look is gone, replaced by a happier one knowing I'm finally (more) comfortable in my own skin. The walls you've spent years building are about to come down. You can exhale now.

Coming out will also show you what true friendship looks like. Some of your closest friends know what's about to happen and they'll always support you. Sadly, though, not everyone will still be here in nine years. So, please treasure your time with them, it's precious. In 2020, a global pandemic will stop people from seeing each other in person for large swathes of time. Firstly, do what you can now to raise the alarm (don't be surprised if nobody pays attention) and secondly, make sure you make up for that lost time together as soon as you can. Don't do what I did and miss out on chances – the pain, the tears and the regret are simply not worth it.

As well as your current friends, the path you're on will introduce you to new friends, all of whom are going to help you to become the better version of yourself who is writing to you now. People who show you how to be a part of the LGBTQIA+ community and how to care for your queer siblings from every hue of the rainbow. You're going to discover things about yourself you never knew existed.

When it comes to relationships, I'm currently single and very happy that way! After many years I've freed myself from the expectation and idea that you need to be in a relationship to be happy. And as with most things, it'll take time, but the freedom will open you to new forms of pleasure and connection that will be so enriching and enable you to create strong bonds between you and others.

Sadly, though, life now isn't easy as an LGBTQIA+ person. I wish I could tell you otherwise, but again, I want to be honest with you. In 2025 you can be gay (or queer), but you can also somehow be 'too gay/queer' or 'not gay/queer enough'. You're encouraged to live out and proud, but don't do it too much because that would be shoving it in other people's faces. You're meant to feel like society accepts you for who you are but a lot of the time you're made to feel slightly estranged. You grow up not always being given the love and support that you need as a queer person, so you start to seek that love and validation elsewhere. However, if you go after it too hard, you're seen as 'needy'. And if you're rejected the cycle continues. And if you don't pursue love you're made to feel like you're incapable of it.

As a community you oppose having labels put on you and being judged by a heteronormative society but then you freely impose labels on and judge subsets of your own community. You can have 'fun', but you're branded 'a slut' for having too much 'fun'. You can enjoy being a supposedly free member of society but then also have your fundamental human rights constantly debated. And you must always be grateful for what you do have. You must always be on guard because if you dress or present 'too queer' then you might be abused or attacked. And if you are, chances are the police won't take your case seriously and nothing will happen. As a community you will forever have to explain why we still need to celebrate

Pride and demand representation in culture and entertainment in the face of constant questioning from people who never seem to listen or want to understand. And on top of that, you can also be criticised by others in your own community for trying to help or defend them because you're somehow doing it wrong, not doing enough, or even doing too much. It's complicated.

Generally, queerphobia is rife across society. After years of progress, governments, companies and organisations are changing their minds about supporting the community and turning their backs on us. Through *Attitude* I've heard from people who've been victims of atrocious crimes and abusive acts. It's heartbreaking, and nothing can quite prepare you for it, but for every step backward and every awful thing that happens, there will be something that shows you just how fiercely the LGBTQIA+ community loves one another, for the most part. There are some in the community who will seek to sow division and unrest, but you must believe there are a great many more seeking to build bridges and support and love.

A key bit of advice from me would be to be bold in everything. For too long I was held back by anxiety and fear, but as I've come to understand personally of late, life is too short to live by those emotions and feelings. Anxiety, especially, has been a big thing for me. Please get help sooner than I did. Start talking to people earlier. In

You're going to meet people who are going to help you become the better version of yourself.

my work as a journalist I've been introduced to people who have experienced the worst traumas imaginable and gone to the depths of where anxiety and depression can lead. I never had it that bad, but inaction is never the answer. The best thing you'll ever do for your mental health is talk to your friends and family about it – you'll be amazed how many of them will empathise with how you feel, and knowing that will lift so much weight from your shoulders.

Just like living with Mum and Dad after university, being a journalist, or even living in Wales for a time, was never in the plan. But it happened. And the only regret I have is that I didn't pursue acting more at your age. I felt scared, you feel scared now – I get it. You've never really had that many big parts and you've the wary voices of your parents, who mean well, in your ears. But honestly, I'm still thinking about wanting to be an actor now and have been picking up classes and joining companies to get back into it. I've spent a bit of every day since I was in your place thinking about it. So, do what you can now! Never stop performing, be it acting or singing – it brings you so much joy and that will only become more valuable as you grow up. You never know where you'll end up and it could be amazing. Don't be ruled by the same fears I was – the regret, as I said earlier, isn't worth it! Remember, be brave, and it'll get you far, regardless.

And if you do stick with the path I've followed, you'll have a great time. You'll be pushed and challenged in ways that will see you grow more and more. Before *Attitude* I worked at the BBC in Wales. Working there is tough; it's a competitive field but you have every right to be there. After all, you have the smarts and know-how to get into one of the best journalism schools in the country, so remember that! But as much as you enjoy broadcasting and getting to see your face on TV or hear yourself on the radio (as well as have others do the same), just remember how much you used to love writing. That will come back to you with *Attitude*. Here, you'll find out what it means to really belong, to work on stuff you love and are passionate about. And finally, you'll feel like you really belong within the LGBTQIA+ community.

It's a brilliant job that will see you chat to all sorts of wonderful and magical people, including heroes of yours such as Sir Ian McKellen (Gandalf! And by the time of writing, we've met three times and on the third, he remembered us from before!), as well as some inspiring people working across the world in all sorts of areas. It's a wonderful combination of professional and personal and will see that you have a platform to help others like you to feel better and less alone than you do now.

I'm jealous of everything that lies before you. The steps from where you are now to here have all been brilliant, wonderful, scary, unexpected and more. You're going to learn so much about yourself and the world. So much also happens culturally in the next nine years, and part of me wants to come back to your time to relive it. You'll also become a keener traveller and some of your most rewarding adventures will be solo ones. First, there's Italy, then Barcelona, Amsterdam – and more are coming. You'll also travel with friends, all of whom you've yet to meet, and you'll have the best time with them too.

I hope all of this has helped. There are many challenges ahead, but you have the strength and the resolve to get through each, otherwise I wouldn't be here writing this now. Just remember that frightened little boy on the school playground, the one who feels an innate sense of 'other-ness' from the other boys and is on his own singing 'Reflection' from *Mulan* or the entirety of Shania Twain's *Come On Over* album, and see how you have grown from that to where you are now. Be comforted by where I am in relation to where you are, the journey in-between. So much is possible – you only have to have faith in yourself and work hard. Love your family and friends, and most importantly yourself, and you'll be just fine.

Love,
Al

Hafsa Qureshi

Activist, Writer and 'Rainbow Muslim'
Bisexual
Any pronouns

Trigger warning: Self-harm

Dear Younger Hafsa,

Breathe. You know that feeling in your chest that feels like a thousand bees and also the bees are on fire? That's called anxiety. Oh, and you're autistic. Surprise! But I'm not writing to you from the future just to give you a health update (though you have a lotta chronic illness in your future, soz). I'm writing to tell you that things got better. It took a while though, so bear with me.

Right now, you wake up every single day wishing that you hadn't. You care for both your parents and it really sucks. Between school and meds, fighting with siblings, food and bills, you're a ball of stress. And among all this, there's this girl. You're going to keep acting like she's not a big deal to you, but we both know that's not true. Your friends talk about the boys at school and you have no idea what they're talking about. They want to get married and have babies with some boy with spiky, gelled Sonic the Hedgehog hair and you don't get it. At my age, you still won't, but let's not get sidetracked. There's this girl. She's cool and pretty and it's not that you want to be like her but more like … You want to be with …? And you're going to avoid finishing that sentence, aren't you?

You can't think about this, you have mountains of homework to do! But homework won't matter when you get older, trust me. But that girl, she will. Because she's the first girl you liked. Like-liked. I know. Deep down, you already knew that, though. And you're not ready to deal with all that, are you? It's a lot to deal with. Want to know the worst part? You're not even going to think about it for years and years. Because … and I'm so sorry to tell you this: they die. Both of them. Our parents, the people you've been caring for, for what feels like forever. They die and it will be the worst thing that ever happens to you. And it still is.

Wait. I know you want to despair right now. Or worse, self-harm. Possibly even end it right now. Just listen. Yes, it was – and is – the worst feeling in the entire world. You won't know what to do afterwards. You won't know how to live. You'll eat cereal for months because you just have no idea how you're supposed to function. So why the hell didn't I lead with that, why am I talking about that girl?!

Letters to My Younger Queer Self

Just wait. Think about it for a second. If I'm sending you this letter that means we're still alive. I wanted to tell you: we didn't just survive this, we overcame it. We became the person our parents always hoped we'd be. We're outgoing, confident, we dress super colourful, we love and are loved in return, we smile all the time, we have a nice job, we're openly bisexual and Muslim ... I can hear the record scratch in your head.

Yeah. You're not going to hear this right now. You're still not willing to admit you even like that girl. And there's no way you'd give up your faith for something so worldly and stupid, right? First off, emotions are great and you're going to learn how to feel them. In front of other people. It'll take time, but you'll stop bottling everything up all the darn time. Well, mostly. Second, I never said you had to choose. You're going to struggle with the thought of it at first. Surely everyone who's gay ends up drinking and doing drugs, renouncing religion and their life is over? (I cannot wait for you to get better friends ...) And wait, bisexual? But you like women! So, you admit it then? Heh.

I don't have time to unpack all of your thoughts, but I'll start with us being bi. Men aren't actually that gross. That's it. Maybe it was the hedgehog hair that was so off-putting. Also, non-binary people exist and you're genderqueer in the future. More surprises! As you get

Your edgy phase of hating everyone and never smiling has an expiration date. You're going to learn that losing the people you cared most for in the entire world does something to your brain.

older you'll discover that you're not just attracted to women – you like all people, really. Yup, you heard me. Your edgy phase of hating everyone and never smiling has an expiration date. You're going to learn that losing the people you cared most for in the entire world does something to your brain. It makes you completely stop giving a damn what other people think. Like the small but ferocious honey badger, you will be filled with apathy for others' opinions of you. And that includes anyone that says you can't be bi and Muslim.

Let's backtrack a bit. So, when the big horrible thing happens, you have to get a job. You won't get to go to university, or follow any of the weird little plans we had all mapped out since we could write. You'll have bills and a mortgage and this part will also completely suck. You're going to work some jobs you hate until you find a stable job that's sort of OK. And then that honey badger attitude kicks in. You join your workplace LGBTQIA+ network because you can and no one can stop you. You meet some really cool people and you hear their stories. And, shock horror, you meet other queer Muslims.

Awesome folks that don't have the privilege of being as out as you are. People that have to hide who they really are or risk losing everything. Here's your reason to stick around. It's not that people need you, but you have a special privilege that some queer Muslims don't. We will have been through more pain than we may ever face again and we survived. Now's your chance to be there for people just like you and tell them that they have a shot at making it out of the darkness too. That they don't have to choose between who they really are and who people wished they were.

You're probably feeling emotional right now, as I am writing this. You might be trying to hide instead of wearing your heart on your sleeve. My advice to you is to let people see the real you, the absolute dweeb that feels so much all the time. Don't crush who you are to fit what other people like. The right people will like you just as you are, weirdness and all. Use that strong sense of justice you have towards making things a bit less terrible in this world, get involved in any way you can. Whether that's through volunteering, social media, or protesting. I know you can do it. I believe in you, even if you don't believe in yourself just yet. Keep going.

Love,
Future Hafsa

Sarah Savage

Activist and Founder of Trans Pride Brighton
Trans
She/Her

Dear Younger Me,

I wish I could stand beside you right now and tell you that the fire burning inside you is a force to be reckoned with, that everything you're feeling is valid and worth pursuing with the same tenacity that you have used to build your double life so far. All those people who will drop you like a stone when you leave their cult are not worth the tears you will shed.

Some good people will say some terrible things to you, but in twenty years, they too will come to wish they had escaped just like you will. The relief that you will feel when you realise that leaving means you no longer have to expend so much energy living that double life will turbocharge the drive and desire to fully experience the world, which you already have.

You may not realise it yet, but the strength you've shown just to survive is extraordinary. I know the grip that cult had on you, how it tried to break you, to convince you that your worth was tied to its twisted beliefs. But let me tell you something: you were never theirs to control. Even in the darkest moments when self-doubt caused you to lie in bed filled with existential dread, praying for the strength to conform, wishing that you could change who you are, there was a part of you that refused to be silenced, that knew deep down you deserved more. That part of you is more powerful than you can imagine right now, and it's what will save you.

You will escape, and that is a victory like no other. You have already defied a system designed to crush you, to strip you of your identity, your autonomy, your very sense of self. But here you are, stronger, wiser and freer than you've ever been. The fact that you broke away, that you chose your truth over their lies, is proof that nothing can stop you, nothing can hold you back and the light inside of you is undimmable.

It is not your fault that your birth parents and siblings are still in the throes of that cult's control and it is not your responsibility to free them from it. You will learn that the idea of family is a construct and you will find a new family who truly love and support you unconditionally, no matter how you dress, who you love and whatever your dreams will become. You are worthy of happiness, of acceptance, of being seen and loved for who you truly are. Don't be afraid to seek out the things that bring you joy, to surround yourself with people who lift you up, who inspire you, and to speak your truth, even when your voice trembles – especially when your voice trembles.

The road ahead won't always be easy. There will be physical and mental scars, memories that haunt you and moments when the weight of what you've been through feels overwhelming. But know this: you will do the impossible. You've already proven that you won't let anyone dictate who you are or what you believe. You are a survivor and that means you have the strength to face whatever comes next, no matter how big the challenges seem to be.

Don't ignore what you've always known to be true, those feelings that your internal gender isn't how everyone else perceives it are valid and worth exploring. Transition isn't a race but you have to show up at the start line, you have to be honest with yourself and you cannot allow yourself to hold back parts of your identity because of your fear of how the world will react. You will face obstacles, people who don't understand, systems that try to erase you and moments of doubt that feel overwhelming. But let me tell you something: you are stronger than all of it. Your identity is not up for debate. You know who you are, even if the world around you

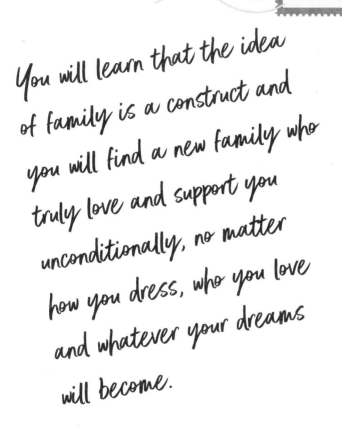

You will learn that the idea of family is a construct and you will find a new family who truly love and support you unconditionally, no matter how you dress, who you love and whatever your dreams will become.

refuses to acknowledge it. You're a warrior, a trailblazer, and you won't let anyone take that from you.

It's OK to feel scared, fear is natural. But never let it stop you. You will face those fears head-on, and in doing so, you'll become the woman you're destined to be. Transition is a journey, one that requires grit, determination and an unshakeable belief in yourself. And guess what? You've already got all of that and more. Every battle you fight, every victory you claim, is proof of your resilience. The life you will build, the people you will inspire, you can start that journey today. There will be so much joy, moments when you look in the mirror and finally see the person you've always known yourself to be. The people who truly matter will love you for you, no conditions, no compromises. And those who don't? They don't deserve to be part of your story. Your life is yours to live, on your terms, without apology. You will finally be truly free and that freedom is something you will have earned. You get to decide what your life looks like from here on out.

You get to choose who you are, who you surround yourself with and how you live. And let me tell you, you deserve nothing less than everything that makes you feel alive, safe and loved. So, keep pushing forward, keep embracing your truth, and keep defying anyone or anything that tries to hold you back. The world may still throw challenges your way, but you've already proven that you're unstoppable. You're not defined by where you came from, but by the strength it took to leave it behind. You're going to make it through this. And one day, you will look back with so much pride at the journey you've taken, at the strength you've shown and at the woman you will grow up to become. Never give up hope, keep believing in yourself and know that you are beautiful, inside and out.

You're going to make it through this. You are powerful. You are resilient. Stand proud, stand defiant and know that you are unstoppable, know that you are so much more than they ever wanted you to believe.

With all the fire and pride and love in the world,

Your Future Self

Dr James Greenwood

TV Vet and Author
Gay
He/Him

Dear James,

    Of all things, know that none of this is your fault. This is just you (or rather 'us', as truly, I'm writing this letter to both you and I).

    Do you remember the days when we would free-fall into yet another unrequited, silent, suffocating crush? Time after time, we'd mull over an imaginary dream without a single word muttered to anyone. The boys that made your heart skip a beat, and sometimes girls, although the dots always found a way to connect themselves a little more fully when the boys walked past. You'd beat yourself up and swear to yourself that you'd never tell a single soul. Decades of stored curiosity, wondering and desire filled your head and your heart with lingering intrigue. Like a pro you managed to keep a lid on it for so many years, although I often look back now and ask, 'to what expense?' as the rumours began to spread.

You've heard (and believed) many things about yourself up to now but let me say to you loud and clear – you're not weird, or unnatural, it's not a 'shame' and you certainly have nothing to be ashamed of. Life won't always seem this hard. You should never have heard those things, nor should they have ever been said. But this 'thing' shall prove itself a learning curve beyond your own individual experience and you are about to learn and unlearn a hell of a lot.

It hurt us both then and it hurts me now to hear the words repeat in your head as you say them over and over. You think crying somehow equates to weakness, of losing. It doesn't. I have lived the life that lies ahead and hindsight tells me that you should cry. You need to cry. Every tear that falls is saturated with the bigotry, ignorance and all the utter bullshit you've heard. Growing up in the eighties and nineties, hurtful words and negative public attitudes towards gay men and women were normalised and they reached your young impressionable mind well before any positive representation or pride. It all makes so much sense to me now, how overwhelmed and confused you feel at present, but I say again – none of this is your fault and you have nothing to feel ashamed of.

Letters to My Younger Queer Self

I can see in your eyes how exhausted, scared and alone you are feeling. My only wish is that I could reach back now and be the person to come forward and stand beside you, to help you through and for us to walk this path together – away from all the sadness and towards the warmth of easier days. But as we both know, this path is yours alone.

From the outside, 'coming out' might seem like the simple flick of a switch, a few small words and life is all sorted out, but you and I both know it's not going to be quite that easy. The path to rock bottom is going to hurt like fucking hell as you tumble down. But from there, when you can't cry anymore, you will suddenly see yourself so clearly: the raw, unfiltered, happy little boy that loved his dog and dressed up in his mother's shoes, sang at the top of his lungs and loved all of life so fully. Take only that version of yourself into the future – you and I are still that person, the projected shame from others is not yours to bare. Don't let it eat away inside you or kill the joy and happiness that life can bring – then, now or in the future.

Everything's a mixed-up mess where you are now. Patience and time will allow the dust to settle and then you'll see what an incredibly brave thing it is that you've just done. For how huge this all feels, it's also not a one-time event. You will come out a thousand times

My only wish is that I could reach back now and be the person to come forward and stand beside you, to help you through and for us to walk this path together — away from all the sadness and towards the warmth of easier days.

more after today. In fact, you will never stop coming out. In the coffee shop, to the hotel receptionist, the postman, the school-gate mums (and dads). Society has moved on in so many ways, but we are still living by default in a 'straight' world. There is a certain 'full circle' irony, though, in that one day you will actually love coming out. You'll get pretty good at it, too. Those with not entirely derogatory but well-ingrained heteronormative presumptions will crack a compassionate self-checking smile when you explain how they have hurtled so confidently towards the wrong conclusion, and then you proudly get to explain your version of 'life'.

Shitty things may be said, but don't use that to beat yourself up or carry the weight of other people's ignorance – don't give them that power, they're a dead weight that will only slow you down through life. Others make honest mistakes, allow them that. You will too and you'll get better at learning to forgive or forget. Stand proud and seek out the intention behind the words you'll hear spoken as well as the words themselves. I do honestly believe there are far, far more good people in this world than there are hateful. Live with the confidence that not everything or everyone is against you. Allow yourself the joy of imagining a future and make it a happy one.

Because from where I am today – with a kind and loving husband, about to light the candles on the first birthday cake for our son – surrounded by all our closest friends and family – I can honestly say with a lived authority that the future is worth sticking around for.

And on today of all days, I am so, so very grateful that you did.

Love,
James

Jamie Windust

Writer, Author and Content Creator
Trans Non-binary
Them/They

Dear Jamie,

 We used to love dance, you and I. Unlike what most people say, we used to dance like everybody was watching – even when they weren't. Even when it was just our reflection watching back, or a handful of girls sitting in the corner of the old tiny dance studio, lined up underneath the ballet bar next to the broken radiator. There was a sense of freedom that came with wanting to do something, and then ... well, doing it! Upon reflection, the concept itself seems almost radical in this day and age, but unbeknownst to us at the time, we were living without shame. Without the fear of judgement.

 So, this letter to you (or me ... I know, it's getting confusing, isn't it?) is from me, the Jamie from the future. Hello! You've got ginger hair still, don't worry. Just perhaps less of it. *Glee* also got cancelled after Season 6, so brace yourself for that.

Anyway, let's get to it.

You're going to hear a lot of blanket statements as you grow up about being yourself and finding out who you really are, but one that I'd make sure to remember is this: Allow the judgement of others to be just that – theirs, and theirs alone. Do not allow it to insidiously prevent you from doing what you want to do. It's not about perfection, it's not about doing whatever you want to do to be better than other people. It's not about them at all. But what I want you to remember is to allow yourself to just give life a go and not let other people's opinions of what you're doing prevent you from grabbing life by the horns, because when you get older, it becomes harder and harder, to do the things you once loved doing. The childhood gay abandon of finding out what makes you happy gets lost and it'll take you a good sixteen years to understand that you can find that freedom again.

The sad truth is you don't end up dancing forever and ever. You don't end up on stage in the West End. You don't end up meeting Harry Styles (yet) or going on tour with the cast of *Glee*. But speaking to you now, Jimbo, the thing that I miss the most about being your age is the fact that your beautiful, blue-sky dreams were never something that you questioned.

As we got older, our dreams became tainted by something called 'societal expectation'. That's the fancy word for it, but one could argue that it's just the poisonous effects of shame on a life once lived in the blissful colour of freedom.

Over time, we became aware of the thoughts of others – firstly, when it came to dance. The adoration you once felt from people applauding and laughing along with your performance turned sinister as you began to question whether or not they were laughing with you or at you. A slow and seeping paranoia began to lay its foundations in the pit of your stomach, making it harder to show up to lessons. The once-innocent eyes of the girls underneath the ballet bar suddenly felt like telescopic lenses, analysing every part of the way your body moved.

So, when you started big school, you stopped. You stopped doing your hair like Justin Bieber too, even after your mum taught you how to use the hair straighteners. Maybe that one was for the best, but either way it became normal for you to question your own desires. Your own instincts or wants were now second-guessed, sometimes third. The music you listened to became something to be laughed at rather than something to huddle round and magically Bluetooth to each other at youth club. Even your love of cooking and watching *Ugly Betty* with your dad on a Sunday afternoon became something that you stopped doing, retreating up to your room to read and eat custard creams – all washed down with a fizzy Vimto.

The boys didn't want to be friends with you anymore and you never understood why. I know now, but I'll spare you the details. Just know that it wasn't your fault. None of it was.

That's what I want to tell you in this letter, amidst the plethora of poncy quotes and silly little rhymes and sayings you'll hear throughout your lifetime on something called Instagram. They'll be about being authentically you or finding your tribe, which is nice and all, but the one thing I want you to really remember is that none of it is your fault. OK?

I think you're the bravest little boy and that's all that matters. Because people aren't going to know how to 'handle' you throughout your life – even all the way up until now, aged twenty-seven. But do you know what? It's not your fault.

It'll be hard, but remember the shame that other people place on your queerness or your transness isn't a reason to not love that part of yourself. Don't let other people's shame poison your chance to live a full, joyous, mistake-laden, colourful life. In the future, your gender changes. Isn't that cool? Like a superhero or like that episode of *Glee* when they all swap places with each other when Tina falls into the fountain and hits her head.

I'm looking into starting dance lessons again and that's all because of you. Because of your childish innocence at just wanting to be good at something you love doing. I love you for that. At wanting to explore a side of yourself that was only motivated by the happiness of movement and the freedom that came with it.

So, although we might not see each other for a while, and there will be some moments when we both don't even recognise each other anymore, know that we will meet again. Even if it's just for a split second when we look in the mirror and catch our reflection, or when we buy ourselves a bottle of Vimto and take that first sip and remember those days hidden away in your bedroom.

Remember, you'll never be alone because I'm right here with you every step of the way. Through thick and thin, highs and lows – I will be here, come what may.

Love,
Jamie

Dating Advice for My Younger Self

Heed Action, Younger You,

Dating etiquette is a minefield. It's horrendous. No one truly follows one rule book, so how on earth are you meant to get it right? You won't get it right – you don't get it right.

If you are single and living in a large city and start dating someone, then they might be dating three other people. Maybe four. And even if you become 'official' that could still be the case. People have evolved and relationships too. Open. Closed. No size fits all.

App dating has helped. App dating has hindered. App dating is toxic. App dating is fantastic.

Kissing someone in a bar or club still feels euphoric. Kiss as many people as you can. Do not shame or be shamed in this. There is nothing wrong with that freedom.

Date kindly, date considerately, don't date, do date, speed date. No, don't ever speed date.

Fall in love until you're sick to the stomach. Fall in love again. Get your heart broken. Break a heart. Mend a heart. Save a heart.

Date yourself.

Letters to My Younger Queer Self

Have sex on the first date, no date, second date … or don't have sex at all.

Dating is a beast; it forever will be. And, if this is a hand that you are dealt – as many times as the dealer decides it – do me a favour, enjoy it.

You might not date forever. You might not want to date forever. They might not want to date you.

You don't have to have a third date rule. You don't have to have any rule.

So, date how you want to date.

Stop being a sheep.

There is no rule.

David Atherton

Baker, Podcaster and TV Personality
Gay
He/Him

Little David,

(And you are little, don't worry about getting measured by the school nurse each and every week, you will eventually go through puberty and be regular-ish size.)

First of all, I want to say how much I love you and how proud I am of you! I know that at this point in your life you're experiencing a lot of self-hate (if you can ease off this just a bit it'll help with untangling your internalised homophobia later), but you are so strong and brave. I love that you continue to go to ballet classes, wear eye liner, knit and bake, even though these aren't popular activities in Whitby, to say the least. Your authenticity is your greatest strength, and your willingness to do things you love even when they're not popular will mean that even though you keep your sexuality hidden for a long time, you won't feel like you've lived a lie.

Secondly, talking about doing things you love, please keep baking. You can't imagine how useful this will be later in life.

Thirdly, something called the internet is going to come into the world and it will be a great tool for you. It's very hard to explain what it is and you wouldn't believe me if I tried. Right now, I know that you're trying to navigate your queerness alone with no one to speak to, but the internet will provide such a wealth of information from amazing queer people with so much experience. One thing I can tell you now, that will hopefully help you, is that being 'gay' is not a binary. There is no such thing as 'straight' and 'gay', and while it was helpful in initially fighting for the right to be equal, eventually people will not be squeezed into boxes and everyone will be celebrated for their uniqueness.

Also, please try harder with your French homework – no one likes a monolinguist.

Finally, dream big.

You don't think it's possible, and you might find it hard to believe, but living happily married with the husband of your dreams, being able to hold hands in public and being fully accepted by your family are on the cards. Honestly, it still seems unbelievable to me now. Some amazing, strong and spirited queers will fight long, hard and successfully to ensure this is possible in the UK and you

Your authenticity is your greatest strength, and your willingness to do things you love even when they're not popular will mean that even though you keep your sexuality hidden for a long time, you won't feel like you've lived a lie.

Letters to My Younger Queer Self

will reap the rewards. Love not hate, this has to be your mantra, and if you can find it in yourself to come out a little earlier, you should do this for others. Coming out won't be as scary as you think it is, it will be empowering. Most importantly, the more queer people who come out and live authentically, the more queer people still in the closet will see and find the strength to come out also.

OK, this really is the final part now. Soon, you're going to want to dye your hair black, but take it from me now (I still have the photos), it doesn't look good, then or now.

Love,
David

Anonymous
A Letter from an Ally, in Reflection

Personally, and as wrong as this may sound now, knowing what I know in my adult life, but growing up as a straight guy, didn't seem, or wasn't seen as a privilege. I guess that shows the ignorance of growing up 'straight'.

A fact, at the time, you're not even aware of.

Privilege.

Growing up, I just felt like I was a part of society and 'the norm'. I went to school, had friends, girlfriends and went to house parties. It all seemed pretty standard stuff. It wasn't until my mid-twenties when my cousin came out that there was a shift in my mindset. At the time, I didn't understand why he came out so late. Looking back, most people within our friendship circle and family thought he was gay and always had been. It triggered something and I couldn't help but reflect back on my own childhood and think about my contribution to the topic of homophobia. I felt guilty for potentially, and thoughtlessly, contributing to what might have been a part of holding him back.

In school, it was 'funny' to call someone gay, faggot or a queer. Those words were thrown around carelessly and, admittedly, they often came out of my mouth. It's shameful to say that I said them. Whoever those words were recklessly thrown at, I don't doubt that they would have contributed to inflicting a negative barrier between heterosexual and homosexual people. After my cousin came out, I realised that society had not made it easy for him. I watched those words commonly spoken on TV shows, leaving the mouths of my family members, daily, and forming part of the local dialect among kids I used to hang out with. I couldn't, and didn't, see the harm that they could cause to anyone.

I was wrong.

My ignorance became a part of the problem.

I spent all of my childhood with my cousin, someone that I love greatly. We grew up together, I looked up to him. Yet, unknowingly, we had experienced school so differently. He was way smarter than me at school, he worked hard, got good grades, he was good at everything, but socially, he couldn't truly be himself because he didn't feel like he could be accepted as easily as I was. That's fucked up. He had to navigate that alone.

Privilege.

Now in our thirties, I'm very fortunate to say that I've met some incredible people within the LGBTQIA+ community who are doing amazing things such as writing books, podcasts, TV appearances and drag performances. All of which inspire me to do better and to be better. I'm also very proud to say that one of my greatest friends wrote this book and that his last book encouraged me to speak openly to my cousin about his experiences.

It's only now that I can see how privileged I was.

Even in this day and age, I see judgement and hear comments which are hurtful and are damaging to many people. And because of this, I can still see how hard it will be for others, like my cousin, to come out and be accepted in society today and be themselves. I recognise many errors in humanity that are still drilled into the masses of ignorant straight men who follow the same old grey and dusty path that was laid down by the generation before them. It's time to rip it up and lay down a new one – with some colour.

I think it's important to recognise these behaviours in people and call them out at every opportunity. Let's educate each other and change for the better.

Now.

Love x

Dave Cooper

DJ and Presenter
Gay
He/Him

Dear Faggot, Batty Boy, Bender, Queer,

Knowing you as I do, darling, you'll read some of these words intently, considerately and no doubt repeatedly. You'll pause while reading along and imagine yourself in infinite situations, looking to prepare yourself as best you can for these hypothetical scenarios which may or may not manifest themselves in your known reality. The outcome of this mental preparation may lead you to avoid some of these pre-conceived scenarios altogether, or conversely, push your cerebral and physical capacities to extremes – neither you nor I can predict what sort of reaction certain situations may elicit from you, but I hope to impart some knowledge to keep you out of harm's way at the very least.

If my memory serves me well enough, you'll spend a lot of your solitary thinking time confused about the world people have created. The spoken and unspoken languages that don't always quite make sense because you can't guess what people really mean, despite being expected to and everyone else seemingly able to. At school, everyone seems to reckon you're gay when you've got no idea yourself (a stiff breeze coming through the window on a hot day gets you going at this point, let's be honest). And even if you knew what your sexuality was yet, when someone in class calls you a faggot, batty boy, bender (you'll grow to love this word), queer (this too, but to a lesser degree) or something else grotesque, you might be sent out of the class rather than the repressed arsehole who yelled it at you.

Why would you want to be OK with being something that gets you removed from the class? 'But it's for your own safety, David,' they'll assure you. It might be because the teacher is a dickhead and agrees with them, or even better, because the law currently says they can't defend you and say it's OK to be gay. It's worth noting here that some things like laws will change and some won't, like people's attitudes. You can't always have a say in what does, but you can control how you perceive and react in these situations. There are other factors that can change too, like some of the lads who call you those names and beat you up – one or two of them might just be screaming yours or another bloke's name into a pillow one day.

Letters to My Younger Queer Self

That's one bit of information I wish I'd known and understood better at school. I could sit here and try to hark back to other individual situations which I wished I'd handled better and try to prepare you for it so you can re-do it on my behalf. However, I've spent too much time in my adulthood worrying about the past and hypothetical future and not making the most of now so I wouldn't ask you to do the same. It's so easy to say things like *'carpe diem'*, 'live in the moment', 'be present' and all the rest of it, but what if your brain chemistry makes you prone to worrying and over-thinking? The thing is, that like most things, it takes practice and I've found that it comes down to how and what you prioritise in life.

Firstly, I'd advise that you learn to view your time as incredibly valuable. Often people don't learn this lesson until later in life when their loved ones start dying, and particularly when they die younger than expected. It's a shock to the system which makes us question our own mortality and how we choose to pass the time on this chaotic space rock. Once you've added a value to your time, what then becomes worth trading it in for? I've found that there's only one thing for me, and the sooner you learn this lesson, the better: it's happiness.

Sounds obvious, doesn't it? I remember Mum saying this when we did our family history project in Year 6 and we had to ask all our family members what they wanted most out of life. 'To be happy and healthy,' was her answer. I remember us rolling our eyes or some similar reaction, but as I've gotten older, it's made more and more sense with each year. After years dealing with anxiety, depression and, as I later found out, undiagnosed ADHD (the triple threat for gays and theys), I learned that instead of prioritising the pursuit of a goal or dream which I assumed would make me happy, it made more sense to prioritise my actual happiness.

I can hear you now, 'So what, you just abandon all goals and don't have any ambitions?' No, diva. Not unless that's what makes you happy, of course. Everyone is different, but let's assume that you turn out to be just like or very similar to this version of me and you'll become the sort of person who wants to try everything and finds it difficult to know what to focus on. If your overriding goal is your inner happiness, this will guide you. It's a seemingly oversimplified goal but nonetheless a valid one, which like any other has its own challenges and vulnerabilities which can see you blown off course in your quest for true happiness and self-actualisation. To help prepare you, I've identified three distractions (there are many others, of course) which will be ever-present and more often than not, will serve to derail your train to Happyville: Money, Status and Power.

I hope you come to realise the same lesson I've learned, which is that money, power and status don't have the same personal worth as they might do in society if you're not happy.

Years from now you'll find yourself working in an airport (super camp, super gay, you'll love it), where you'll get to meet people from all over the world with incredible stories to tell. There was a semi-regular story which I'd hear from people who arrived at my check-in desk with one-way flights to somewhere far away. They'd tell me that they'd spent their life chasing a dream career, working their way to the top of some company, pouring money into an expensive house and buying designer clothes and whatever else they were told by society they needed in order to to be content with their life. After a number of years, they realised that they were deeply unhappy, often because they'd decided early on to attach themselves to a particular career goal. It might be that they'd trained and studied with this career in mind and had thoughts that it would bring them one or more of the three things I mentioned above. They'd perhaps dreamed of earning lots of money, which they could use to buy lots of nice things and build a comfortable and secure life in an unpredictable world. They'd earn respect with a fancy job title, impress those at family gatherings or business mixers, or even have the right to a few extra letters which they could write before or after their name. They might even be at the top of a hierarchical management structure where they could wield power and influence, maybe even change the world depending on the existence of any altruistic tendencies.

It was these people who would talk to me and explain what they'd done with their life so far while I did the menial but enjoyable tasks of swiping passports and checking they had the right visa (much to the annoyance of those queuing in the VIP lanes behind them). Often, they'd achieved their goals of earning a mixture of money, power and status, but it seemed to have come at a regrettable cost. Perhaps they'd lost a marriage or long-term partner due to their fixation on other things, not spent enough time with loved ones before they passed away, or watched their children grow up. Some said they'd got to the top of their game but were surrounded by self-serving, back-stabbing phoneys who weren't there to celebrate their perceived success but rather to try to tear them down. The pressure of society made them marry someone of the opposite sex and have children, while all the time they were homosexual and only had the courage to live honestly later in life. Hearing stories like this over the years has cemented my view that while money, power and status obviously have their uses in a chaotic world, they're not the things that people wish they'd had more of when confronted with their own mortality. Don't get it twisted, you should remain aware that for most people on our planet the world demands that we participate in some form of civilised society in which these three things seem to dominate. Some misunderstand and think I'm suggesting we abandon all pursuits of the former in some form of radical social rejection of society at large. That said, I hope you come to realise the same lesson I've learned, which is that money, power and status don't have the same personal worth as they might do in society if you're not happy.

So how do you make that happen?

I'm afraid happiness isn't automatic either, unfortunately, which is another cruel lesson we all seem to have to learn in our own time. Making decisions and choices which put your happiness first may not guarantee it to you, or that it will stay with you. Much like money, status and power, it can come and go over time or even in an instant. My belief right now is that if you prioritise it and let it guide your decision-making as much as possible (you'll still have to work if you want to eat and party, my dear, there's no getting out of that), then you've got a much better chance of making it through to the bitter end in one piece, perhaps even with a smile on your face, knowing that you did your best.

Love,
Dave

Stu Oakley

Parent, Author and Podcaster
Gay
He/Him

Trigger warning: Mental health conditions, body dysmorphia

Dear Stuart,

First things first, let me say one thing: I'm sorry. I'm really sorry that over the years I've treated you so badly. We had a turbulent time together, you and I, and it's taken me quite some time to really address things.

You'll laugh, but I now go by the not-hugely drastically different name of 'Stu' and if anyone calls me 'Stuart', I go all prickly and defensive like a cat caught down an alley by a stray dog. My colleagues at work used to chuckle when I'd go bright red with anger if someone called me Stuart in an email, but during one particularly enlightening therapy session I realised that by adamantly switching to just 'Stu' at university and beyond, I was essentially severing ties with you. I don't think it will surprise you, but I didn't like you very much. I wanted to escape you. You were fat, you were emotionally unstable, confused, camp, annoying, and I tried everything I could to distance myself from that little boy without addressing who I actually was and what I wanted in life. I'm sorry that I've been so unkind to you. You'll be happy to know I now have children, as I remember this always being a hope of yours. Now I'm a parent I just can't imagine being as cruel to my own children as I was to you. It's easy for me to say now, but you've got to start being kinder to yourself, you've got to start to learn how to love yourself and own who you are. You have to understand that the abuse you suffered, and that I don't need to repeat here, was not your fault: you were so young, and no blame should lie with you. Again, easier said than done when looking back. And on top of all the shit you were dealing with, you were also trying to figure out who you were and what it meant to be gay in the world.

You may have noticed me mentioning therapy. The biggest regret you will have in life is not starting it earlier. How I wish you'd find someone to talk to. You're bottling it all in, and starting a relationship at the age of fourteen with a boy who wants it to be secret is not going to help matters. You're going to get more and more frustrated, and that frustration will come out as anger towards those closest to you, including your secret boyfriend. It's a vicious cycle and one I hoped you'd escape sooner than you did. Loving with all your heart, and then falling too hard, is both your greatest strength and your biggest weakness in life, love and even your career. I've always remembered you as obsessive and controlling, but perhaps now I see that you just loved the 'boy'. And with so little other control in your life, you wanted to make that relationship as special as it could be. I'll tell you now, it never worked out. In fact, it ended very quickly, and very fiercely, after a teenage screaming match outside a Sainsbury's before you started your shift on the trolleys, and it's been almost twenty-five years since the last time you saw or spoke to him. But do not fear: at the tender age of sixteen, it didn't break your heart as much as you thought it had at the time. It made you stronger and it helped you in your next step to become Stuart 2.0 … well, Stu.

The relationship actually ended only five years before you were to meet your husband. Yes, Stuart, you get snatched up young! But be prepared, you will also go through a few years of getting desperately sad and anxious about being loved before this happens. Your weight and appearance are wrapped up in this for sure. The one thing I wish I could tell you is that the weight issue gets easier, but sadly, it doesn't, as even with a 'Stu' rebrand and a five-stone weight loss at university, the deep-set eating disorders and body dysmorphia have

Now I'm a parent I just can't imagine being as cruel to my own children as I was to you. It's easy for me to say now, but you've got to start being kinder to yourself, you've got to start to learn how to love yourself and own who you are.

become part of you. This is why I again so wish you'd had the right help at the beginning. If you had grown up today, I hope that you might have had more access to support or guidance and that you didn't follow a path of self-destruction when it came to your body. But everything I wished for you I now have hope for my kids. We, you and I, have three – a girl and two boys, you'd love them. They are my world. You used to worry that perhaps being gay might stop you from having children, but I'll say to you what I say to my daughter now: anyone can have a child if they really want one. Obviously for queer people things can sometimes be more than just a little complicated, but if you are determined that children are part of your future, then go for it.

We (my husband John, you'd love him too) decided to adopt. It was by no means a super-easy process, but no way was it as arduous, invasive and stressful as some people may think. It's obviously different for everyone, but we had a really positive experience and it actually allowed me to question and explore you before I made that step of becoming a parent. Not many have that luxury. The older they get, the more and more I reflect back on your experiences as a teenager. And as we race towards the teenage years, I never, ever want them to feel the shame that you did about yourself, and I hope that your experience will have taught me to be conscious and aware of signs that things are not OK. As an adoptive parent I have had this drilled into me anyway because of the training and focus you are given on therapeutic parenting, but I hope your trauma at least gives me an edge. I want them to be happy and confident about the body they have, whatever its shape. I want them to connect to like-minded others, and while social media can be a curse, I hope they can use it when needed to find their own tribe quicker than I ever did.

I wish you'd known more gay people, or any gay people for that matter. I think being the only obviously gay person at school made you incredibly lonely and added to the intense frustrations. Your 'boyfriend' was so confused that he was never someone you could lean on to help you understand you. Young people need people around them to help them work out who they are and I'm so glad that people today get that more than they did before. It makes me hopeful that my children will grow up in a world that, for all its faults, allows you to find one another and connect with someone. So, Stuart, I'm sorry. I'm sorry that I wanted to cut you out of my life and try and forget you. You are me, and I was you. You were an amazing young boy filled with love, passion and, yes, cake. But you survived. You grew up to be me, and despite some ups and downs, I do like me. I like *us*. Hopefully, now is the time for you to love yourself. After all, we have three incredible humans to now look after. Come, take my hand and let's go and kick parenting ass together.

I love you.

Stu(art) x

Tom Aspaul

Singer
Gay
He/Him

Dear Tom,

You're thirty-eight now. It's a bit weird to think that you're canonically older than Marge Simpson or two years older than Princess Diana ever was. You're the same age as Barbra Streisand when she released *Guilty*. That's a lot to live up to. And sometimes you think to yourself – 'oh my God, I could have had a baby when I was twenty and they would be going to university this year, what the fuck?' And although these thoughts do occasionally creep in, on the whole, getting older doesn't really seem to matter that much.

At least not for someone like you.

I bet you'd never in a million years think that you'd still be living with your parents at thirty-eight. Not to say you didn't live away from home for nearly twenty years, but being a creative person and living in London eventually becomes unbearable, so back home to where it all began you go. Maybe when you were in your twenties you'd have been mortified by this prospect, but actually, take a deep breath and have a think – this is the life that makes sense right now. And you're having a ball (mostly!).

Touring the world is fun, go-go dancing is fun, writing songs is fun, performing all throughout the year is fun! But being thirty-eight does actually mean a lot of random aches and pains, it's true what they say. You cannot keep up quite as much with the younger folks as you used to. But who cares?

You're the best you have ever looked. Your skin doesn't show any sign of ageing. Your hairline remains intact. But unlike these kids, you have several lifetimes, more experience under your belt than they do. You've done nearly every kind of job. You've travelled the globe, lived in different countries, cities. You've loved and lost. You've grieved. You've grown. You're at ease with who you are and that shows. All the hang-ups, self-sabotaging and insecurities all but disappeared once you crossed over thirty.

You still notice people staring, looking, pointing at you in your small suburban neighbourhood. On the train. At the supermarket. Even in the big city. If this was 2002 it would have destroyed you, pushed you further into the closet, perhaps so far inside you'd have never made it out. But here we are in 2024 and you just look and laugh right back.

Keep going. Keep not giving a shit, and be thankful every day that you made it, because not everyone did. If only there were people like you around to look up to when you were younger.

Love,
Tom

Sean Saifa Wall

Activist and Scholar
Intersex

Trigger warning: Trauma, abuse, sexual abuse, death

Dear Susanne,

Before you would receive letters from lovers and partners, your father wrote letters from prison to you, your mother and your siblings. Those letters contained longings for freedom and sweet words to compensate for an absent father. In the same vein as your father's letters, I am writing this letter to remind you of how much you are loved, seen and witnessed. In addition, I hope that some of these words allow your soul to both rest and heal.

One time my friend, Tre, posted on social media …

'You survived so much and survived so little.'

I am now forty-five, speaking to you at fourteen. Your body has changed. At thirty-five, I got a bit of a belly that hasn't gone away. Those breasts, created by excess testosterone and made supple by oestrogen and Provera, are gone. You have two scars that almost match the other scars on your belly from the gonadectomy. I know the pain is still fresh in your mind; being hollowed out by the surgeon's knife as he removed your healthy testicles.

They lied to you, Susanne.

Your 'gonads' were testicles that pumped your body with testosterone, which in excess gave you breasts. I wish that Mom would have listened to you when you asked her if you could have both oestrogen and testosterone after surgery. I know that you were curious about the changes happening in your body but weren't opposed to them. You were intrigued by the musculature in your arms and quads, the stubble and the dark shadow across your upper lip. You were ready for those changes but existed in a world that was not ready for you. Your body was so beautiful and they butchered it. I remember how it felt when those muscular thighs became soft and saddled with cellulite; the stubble and hard lines along your jaw and hips starting to smooth out. The surgeon and endocrinologist attempted to fashion your body in preparation for sex with your future husband.

The first moment of agency was when you told the surgeon you did not want him to shave your clitoris and create a cavity inside of you. You honoured your body's wisdom and acknowledged how his words made you feel sick. Your mother, in turn, honoured your decision, which spared you from harmful medical intervention.

Letters to My Younger Queer Self

That moment would mark the first of many decisions towards your fight for body autonomy.

As I am speaking to you, Susanne, I want to acknowledge a few moments in your life that were devastating but profoundly shaped the person you are today.

Your being molested was not your fault.

In that situation where the cab driver touched you inappropriately, you immediately moved out of harm's way. You were holding the cab while your father was in the check-cashing place. You felt uncomfortable with how the man was looking at you in the rear-view mirror. Even when he started massaging your legs, it felt good at first until he touched your private area. You kept silent when your intoxicated father returned to the vehicle because you were trying to manage a situation where if you told him what had happened he would have tried to murder that man. You should not have had to navigate that situation as a child – you deserved protection and a sober father who would not have left you alone with a grown man.

Speaking of your dad, his choices were the result of lifelong emotional pain and trauma. As I began my healing journey for us, I confronted similar issues with addiction that mirrored our father. I probably got drunk three times in my life and weed made me sleepy, but my addiction to unavailable women, porn and masturbation made my life unmanageable at one point. Eventually,

I see you and you deserve the fucking world.

Letters to My Younger Queer Self

I found support through 12-step programs and therapists who were committed to my recovery and survival.

Twenty-three years after your dad passed, in 1993, your mom died. Nothing could prepare you for the grief. Ever. When your dad died, your mother took the reins of parenting and did the best that she could. She was the youngest girl in her family who survived both sexual assault and racial terror. Her experiences contributed to mental illness that would manifest in paranoia and unfettered rage. She was both loving and harmful – a dynamic that would eventually define some of your romantic relationships. Her death was unexpected and broke your heart.

The year that she died, everything broke, but the breaking-open freed you.

I end this letter by saying that I love you. I see you and you deserve the fucking world. Ignore the people who tease you – they don't see you or know you. Don't let anyone tell you that you can't do anything that you put your mind to. Walk with your head high and always know that you stand on the shoulders of ancestral giants who are always rooting for you on the other side of the veil.

Love,
Saifa

James Barr

Comedian, Podcaster and Radio Presenter
Gay
He/Him

Trigger warning: Abuse, sexual abuse

Hey little James,

   I'm writing to you from where we are now, in a place where we're thriving, although I know it might not seem that way to you yet. It feels strange writing this letter because I talk to you every time I'm about to perform or face something tough. I always sense your fear of being yourself, afraid of standing out and shouting at me, 'What the hell are you doing?!' This all stems from the bullying we endured for being ginger and later for being gay – and more. I wish the older me could have protected you. I'm sorry I wasn't ready then, but everything you've been through has given me the strength I rely on today. So, thank you for taking care of me and getting us to this point. Just before I step out on stage, I say to you in the mirror, 'I'm here now', 'I've got us', 'We know what we're doing' – and I truly mean this.

Letters to My Younger Queer Self

It's taken a long time for me to be able to connect with you. For most of my adult life, I tried to run away from you or drown you out with drinking. We're a shy, quiet gay boy from Eastbourne who's always been seen as different. We were bullied at school and we went through that awful experience with a boy in our year … and all we ever deserved was love. But in my attempt to protect you, I turned into a loud, proud, opinionated broadcaster and comedian who reaches millions of people performing on stage, on the radio and in angry debates with Piers Morgan.

Honestly, I've put you through hell. You wanted to hide and I dragged you kicking and screaming into the spotlight.

I've been wanting to tell you this for a while now: you didn't deserve the bad things that happened to you. It's not your fault. Being gay can make us vulnerable, but it's not being gay that caused those bad things to happen: they happened because the world around us failed us.

When our school friend Ben* said, 'It's normal,' we believed him. When he said, 'All the other boys are doing this,' we believed him too. And when we told him we didn't want to continue, but he ignored us and persisted, we did everything we could to protect ourselves – it's not our fault

---

*   Name changed.

Honestly, I've put you through hell. You wanted to hide and I dragged you kicking and screaming into the spotlight.

this wasn't enough. It's not our fault we were sexually abused during our three to four years at senior school.

I also want you to understand that this experience did not cause you to be gay. It didn't happen because of your sexuality either. Abuse can happen to anyone, regardless of who you are attracted to. I need you to know this because I've processed it all, yet I can still feel your doubt in everything. It's why we recently settled for much less than we deserve by staying in a violent relationship too long. We accepted mere crumbs, believing our self-worth was so low that we thought violence was normal and that we should shut up because we were fortunate to have found someone who loved us. It saddens me to admit this and I'm not blaming you; I'm explaining it to you. We deserve love, growth and protection, and I write to you from the future to let you know that I am now providing all of those things for you – and that you are safe now.

Love,
James

Adrien Gaubert

Co-founder of myGwork
Gay
He/Him

Hi Adri,

I hope you're enjoying the beauty of our little mountain village, Chanac, in southern France. I want you to know that those feelings that make you feel different are what make you uniquely you, and that's something truly special.

When you head off to Lyon for university, you're stepping into a place where you can finally be yourself. You'll find friends who really get you and who will be there for the laughs and the tough times. They're going to be a huge part of your journey.

When you came out to Mom, her reaction was about her worries for your future, not a lack of love. She was just concerned about the world you'd have to face. Even though she's no longer with us, know that her love never wavered and this tough time will only make you stronger. Unfortunately, you'll come across some rough patches at

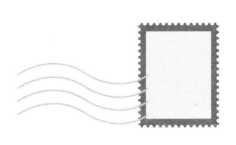

You'll find friends who really get you and who will be there for the laughs and the tough times. They're going to be a huge part of your journey.

work because of who you are. It's not fair, but it will fuel a fire in you and Pierre to start myGwork, creating a safe and inclusive space for others like you. Through this, you'll help tons of people find jobs where they feel welcome and accepted.

Everything's going to be OK. MyGwork will be successful, and you and Pierre will make a real difference in people's lives. You'll also stay close to your brothers, Pierre and Valentin, and will visit Chanac together often.

Your adventure won't stop there. You'll move to Paris, China, Mexico and London, where you'll meet the most incredible people who will open your eyes and change how you see the world. Those experiences will be transformative, adding richness and perspective to your life.

After you hit thirty, you'll really start finding your true self and learn to be kind to yourself – which is so important. You will also have the opportunity to give unconditional love to a child, Sofia, your god-daughter.

Remember, you're never alone. You've got your brothers, your friends and your community standing by you every step of the way. Your journey is yours and every part of it is shaping you into the amazing person you're meant to be.

With lots of love,
Adri

Paris Munro

Radio Presenter
Trans
He/Him

Dear Younger Me,

You're still here ... Can you believe it? I know it's confusing, and you realised from a very young age that something was different about you ... There's so much to learn about yourself.

You have an ongoing journey with your sexuality and your identity, and that's OK. You're growing up through Section 28, which is hard enough, and there will be dark days, but I promise you'll get through it – you're surrounded by people who love you, and love is priceless and the most precious thing in the world.

It gets better.

You are the happiest you've ever been and everything that you imagined came to life ... You get to be your true self FINALLY after thirty-odd years. You can feel the sun on your chest, feel the hairs on your face, and you have the most incredible person in the world who supports you through this entire journey.

Please don't give into the dark days ... Like anything, everything is only temporary.

Don't give up.

Learn, love, laugh, be curious, and don't be afraid to just go for it.

Love

Paris
Your True Self

Andrew Donaldson-Wheatcroft

Digital Creator
Gay
He/Him

Andrew Wheatcroft
Some street in Pinxton
Derbyshire, UK

Dear little Andrew,

    It's 37-year-old Andrew here. I know this is weird. I promise this is good news so don't throw this letter away just yet, it's not a joke! I've got something to tell you.

    Where shall we begin? Let's take a deep breath. It's probably best if we start at the beginning, isn't it? Always a good place to start. Growing up for you will be a weird mix of emotions: you will sometimes feel like you don't fit in and you know what? That's perfectly fine and I really promise it is. You'll find out that not fitting in has given you the best life possible later in life.

You have the best family around you, but you need to speak up if something is wrong and people will help. Don't try and keep it all to yourself when you don't feel 100 per cent, as there's so much help available out there and you need to talk. Talking is what makes you happy later on in life, and I know you probably won't believe this but talking about your thoughts and feelings turns into the best career when you're older! I know this doesn't seem that way at the moment but it's coming – I promise.

Something really terrible happens to you when you're thirteen from someone in the family and I promise you it's not your fault. None of it is ever your fault. You are the strongest little boy that ever lives. You use this trauma and turn it into the most incredible strength to be able to help others and to achieve the life of your dreams. This part of your little life is hard, but I've got you safe when you get older.

When you get to school, you are so shy and you don't know how to handle it, but then you get a voice and you realise how bloody special you are at making people laugh and this becomes your superpower. You get through the hardest years at school by using humour, and later on in life, you get through some of the most difficult times using your humour.

Remember, Andrew, children can be so cruel at times. They don't mean it, it's just kids being kids. Once again this happens because you don't fit in and you don't feel like the rest of the kids and you realise that you don't like the girls in 'that' way, like all the other lads. Am I gay? What does gay even mean? It's such a confusing time and no one you know is gay, and growing up in a small mining town, no one ever talks about people being gay so you don't know how to feel or what to do about it, but I promise being gay is so fucking brilliant! It takes you a little while to understand this, but you wouldn't want to be straight, even if they made you a billionaire.

Your childhood is filled with so many beautiful moments with the most beautiful huge family, but there are so many moments that are traumatic that shape your life as you get older and you don't realise how much until your early thirties, so please be kind to yourself and mindful of how your behaviour impacts others, but it turns out OK and remember that you are not a consequence of someone's actions, it's always a reflection of what they've been through or are going through.

You will go through life not really sure on what to do as a career or how to make money but, little Andrew, please bloody listen to me now and stop wasting your money on shit and spending every last penny, which means you are constantly in debt and nearly bankrupt. You are bloody shit with money, so shit! I would try and give you some advice here, but it was fun, so go wild.

It changes in your thirties, so it's fine, but if you want to listen then do save a little. But I know you won't, so I'll see you with money in the bank at around thirty-two years old.

You go through so many jobs and you do some bad shit which nearly puts you in prison, but this is all part of the healing process with your mental health and the struggles you faced as a kid. You think you aren't wired correctly and in so many bloody ways that's true, but you are always seeking validation because of the trauma which in turn has made you do some bad shit, but you put all the wrongs right later in life and we get you back on track, I promise.

There is one day when it all changes for you, though, and it's all been worth it for this moment. You're going through the deepest darkest times in life and post a random skincare haul on your Instagram just to pass time and hopefully find a new hobby and stick with it, because it will change your entire life and those around you.

That random skincare post has turned into a career, allowing you to live the life you've always dreamed of and to travel the world and tick off your entire bucket list at thirty-seven. Remember that shy gay kid? He's not shy anymore – he walked New York Pride with a skincare brand, he uses his voice to discuss his HIV diagnosis and you have the husband of your dreams living the life you

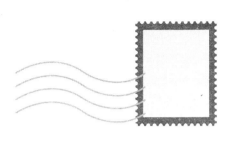

I promise you the world needs you; the world relies on you to make them laugh and to make them smile but, more importantly, other people need to hear your story to realise they are not alone.

deserve but never thought you'd achieve. Actually, wait a minute: that's a lie, you never once doubted yourself. It was always going to happen.

So, little Andrew, listen to me when I say this. The world seems dark and the world seems hard for so, so long and you battle your demons in silence for nearly thirty years, but I promise you the world needs you; the world relies on you to make them laugh and to make them smile but, more importantly, other people need to hear your story to realise they are not alone.

I'm Andrew, I'm thirty-seven and this is for you, little Andrew. We did it. We fucking did it!

Keep going,

Yours sincerely,
Andrew Donaldson-Wheatcroft, aged thirty-seven

Rebecca Swarray

DJ, Curator and Producer
Queer
She/Her

Dear Rebecca,

I remember you with your bushy hair and glasses. A total geek who loved creative writing.

I remember you loving music – especially Mariah Carey and Mary J. Blige.

I remember you not feeling like you fitted in anywhere but at the same time not caring that you didn't.

I remember you making sure you finished every book but always read the ending first.

I remember when you first liked a girl and wondered what all those feelings meant.

I remember you loving a pot of tea and stack of toast and butter on a Sunday morning with Mum, watching *Worzel Gummidge* on Channel 4.

I remember your first broken heart, which wasn't from a first love, but from losing your brother.

Letters to My Younger Queer Self

I remember your strength and resilience through all the low points, too young to comprehend what life had thrown at you.

I remember you having to grow up too fast too soon but learning so much along the way.

I remember you coming out and the beautiful feeling of release and freedom when you did.

I remember you saying goodbye to Mum, but the comfort of being with her until the end.

I remember those years when you didn't know what to do with your life – the struggle was always real.

I remember you praying for guidance in hopeless times. Trying hard to find yourself.

I remember all the limitations they placed on you, but you overcame and overachieved.

I want you to know this: through life experience there isn't a price on your peace of mind, give yourself the grace to find that and when you do, do not compromise it.

Andrew Stamp

Olympic Gymnast
Gay
He/Him

To the little gay Andrew,

    Yes, I called you gay, get over it! Listen up because this might just save you a lot of heartache. You're at the beginning of my journey and you're blissfully naive. Your biggest challenge is not putting your school sweatshirt on inside out and working out how to win the next wrestling match with your siblings. But you're in for one hell of a rollercoaster ride, full of twists and turns.

    You will find your passion at the extremely young age of five. At this age you're a little shit, so Mum and Dad have signed you up to gymnastics as they've had enough of you jumping off the arms of the sofa. In just hoping that you'd burn off the Fruit Shoots, they will inadvertently kick-start a lifelong career as a gymnast that'll take you around the world experiencing a life that few get to see.

Gymnastics will shape your formative years; it will be a part of your childhood and will continue to grow with you as you become a young man. And with anything, it will have its benefits but also its downfalls. Ultimately, nothing will feel like gymnastics. Nothing will feel like flying through the air, the panic of falling on your head and the confidence of getting back up. The excitement of doing a skill for the first time and the effortless bliss of hitting that skill perfectly for the first time. It's the feeling of hitting a golf ball just right but with your whole body (or so I imagine, I've never played golf).

Even at a young age, you've seemingly had an unrelenting drive to thrive on competition. Maybe it's the constant need to prove yourself as good enough despite being gay, but that's another story. In an elite sporting environment, the stakes are even higher. It's a world that champions toughness and strength above all else, where pushing through pain is glorified and where success is often equated with sacrificing every ounce of yourself for the pursuit of greatness. This environment takes a toll on the body and mind, especially as a young gay man. In a hyper-masculine space, where the display of vulnerability is synonymous with weakness, being true to yourself can feel like an insurmountable challenge.

As a gay kid navigating this world, the pressure to conform to traditional notions of masculinity can feel suffocating. The fear of being judged, ostracised or worse can cast a shadow over even the brightest moments of triumph. You learn quickly to hide parts of yourself, to bury your true identity beneath layers of performance and façade. Life becomes about 'Don't look at me, look at what I just achieved'. But in doing so, you lose more than just authenticity, you lose connection. Connection to yourself, to your teammates and to the sport that once brought you joy. The constant battle to suppress your true self drains your energy, leaving you feeling isolated and alone, even in a room full of people, even when they're cheering for your success. The pressure to conform, to fit into a narrow mould of acceptability, will leave scars that may never fully heal. And while the journey to self-acceptance may be long and arduous, it's a journey worth embarking on.

I wish you didn't have to grow up so fast, I wish you had the freedom to explore yourself and I wish you understood what you were feeling. I'm angry at the situations you were put in. You were never seen as a kid, you were old beyond your years and, unfortunately, you were treated as such. You mirror the adults around you because you didn't know how to be yourself. You have become adept at blending into your surroundings, desperate to evade being seen and avoid scrutiny.

I do not regret your decisions – you are fighting as hard as you can and the defences and walls allow you to feel

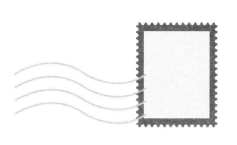

This environment takes a toll on the body and mind, especially as a young gay man. In a hyper-masculine space, where the display of vulnerability is synonymous with weakness, being true to yourself can feel like an insurmountable challenge.

safe, allow you to feel in control. Yet, I recognise now that sometimes the very defences we construct to shield ourselves can inadvertently inflict harm. But there is always hope: never stop fighting, because you have the most amazing family and friends. You'll ring Dad every time you do any kind of DIY because he's still one of those annoying bastards who can do everything – I swear the man knows it all.

Mum is still the strongest person you'll ever meet. Any challenge she can solve, making it seem ten times smaller. She'll keep you up to date with all the hometown gossip and you'll still finish every interaction with an obnoxiously loud and drawn-out 'love you, bye'.

Your brother will always keep you grounded (no matter what you do, you're still the younger brother) and your sister – well, she is still 'always right'. That fact has – and probably never will – change. They're a constant reminder that we are never truly alone, no matter how far we wander from the safety of home. They remind us that we are more than a gymnast, a concept we sometimes lose when at training camps and competitions. Whether we become an Olympian or stop all of it today, we will always be Andrew, and for that I am grateful.

As comforting as the embrace of family may be, there are aspects of our identity that even the most loving parents may struggle to understand. It's in these moments of uncertainty that you'll find the most incredible friends. These people offer a level of connection that might feel foreign at first, but you'll soon come to realise that it's a bond that forms enduring relationships. They're the ones who'll stand by you through the tears – both joyful and sorrowful – and offer unwavering support when you need it most. You'll put the world to rights over your stupid little coffee and stupid little pastries on a Sunday morning. The seemingly most insignificant moments will become some of your most treasured memories. They're our sense of belonging, they'll show you have to love yourself, to love others and to love a man. They're a walking, breathing, talking reminder that you're going to be just fine.

Be patient with yourself as growth is not linear and has no end goal. For every challenge you overcome, there will be another one to tackle. But you do not have to live perfectly and you don't have to have your shit together 24/7. Embracing yourself takes time and I'm still working on it, but if you could start now, it'll make my life much easier. Thanks in advance.

With love, Andrew x

Conor Clark

Journalist – Queer Media
Gay
He/Him

Dear Conor,

Have you ever had someone look at you like you're crazy? Not in the sense that you said something wild or gave a hot piece of gossip, but in an entirely serious, truly concerned-for-your-wellbeing type of way? I have.

On 1 November 2015, I woke up knowing that I would drop out of the university in the cruel town of Winchester I'd been studying at for just seven weeks. I'd had enough. I cannot put into words how unbelievably miserable I was beyond saying that it may have just been the lowest point of my life – and I've had some low points – so that's saying something.

Many of the people around me thought I'd gone off the deep end. They couldn't fathom how, at the age of nineteen, I'd decided to go against the path we'd all spent years being guided towards. But, if there's one thing you should know about me, it's that I've always been stubborn and had faith in my own intuition above all else. So, by lunchtime that day, I'd begun the process of leaving university and I escaped back to London not long after that. It remains the best decision I've ever made.

That choice paved the way for my future in a way I knew it would then and know it did now. In the year that followed, I worked full time at the Jack Wills clothing store on just £6.76 an hour in order to afford fulfilling a lifelong dream of working in and travelling around America. In the summer of 2016, I boarded a plane alone for the first time to work at Camp Homeward Bound, the country's first summer sleep-away camp designed specifically for homeless children.

I felt courage that the 13-year-old me who got bullied for being gay and wearing purple jeans could have only dreamed of. Making such a drastic life change had empowered me and I started to go after what I wanted from life.

I ended up going to a new university which – full disclaimer – had always been my intention. But saying and doing are two different things, which might be why people thought I was crazy when I initially left my first uni. Ironically enough, I ended up attending three universities. That feeling of empowerment from 2015 was with me for every second of my third extended stay in America. I've never felt as fearless, as ready to try anything and everything, as I did during the year I spent in that city. Anyone who knows me has made the 'We get it, you lived in Boston' joke to me at least a dozen times, but I'm self-aware enough to know I still talk about it constantly, so that's OK. You know that too because it's in this letter, but the reality is that none of the good can happen without the bad, and that's why holding onto the good matters.

Fast forward a few years and I'm now an established professional in the LGBTQIA+ media industry, but that didn't happen overnight or without people thinking I'd lost my mind either. Back in 2021, I was offered my literal dream job at *Gay Times* as a junior news reporter (a somewhat bizarre title, given that there was nothing junior about being the magazine's only reporter, but that's a conversation for another day). If you had asked me where I wanted to work when I was a student, I would have said *Gay Times*, no doubt about it. I used to secretly download copies of it onto my Kindle (I couldn't afford an iPad) and delete them so no one would know I was gay – that's how much it meant to me.

So, you might be wondering why people thought I was unhinged to take that job. Well, it's all the result of something most working-class people like myself hate to talk about: money. The pay was just £22,000 for a full-time position, which was – and is – impossible to live on in Central London, as well as being a major decrease in

I felt courage that the 13-year-old me who got bullied for being gay and wearing purple jeans could have only dreamed of.

salary to what I was on while working freelance. But, with me being me, I began to work seven days a week at two jobs simultaneously in order to make it work.

Did I do it because I couldn't afford the role at *Gay Times* without working at LBC radio too? Definitely, but we'd also all just lived through what felt like an eternal lockdown due to COVID-19, much of which I spent being unemployed and broke. I was ready to work and I wanted to prove myself.

I kept both going all the way through to 2024 and throughout those three years there wasn't a single moment when people didn't think I'd gone mad. I'd be asked almost daily how I didn't burn out, how I maintained a social life and where I got the energy from. The truth is, I still don't have an answer to any of those questions, but what I do know is that my drive stemmed from the fact I've never doubted myself. That's not to say I've always got everything right, I certainly haven't, which I was reminded of in March 2024 when I was made redundant from *Gay Times* just a month after quitting LBC.

It felt like the stable ground I'd walked on for three years had shifted beneath me and it happened at a less than ideal time in my personal life, as it always does. That drive of mine held strong though, as I was on Zoom calls to potential employers within thirty minutes of learning I was at risk of losing my job. As my friend Cheryl (the legendary drag queen formally known as Cheryl Hole) told me that week, 'Those you've stood by will return the favour now you need them.' She was right, as she always is, and I had a new job within a week of losing my old one – it's funny the way things work themselves out.

Nonetheless, I've been thinking about my younger self a lot recently because of the U-turn my career suddenly took. Was this really what the me who watched Betty Suarez walk the corridors of *Mode* for the first time in 2006 fought so hard for? An industry full of instability, ruthlessness and nepo babies? One plagued by privilege, where the power is so often held by those who have done nothing to earn it? It's exhausting.

So, while I'm aware that the point of this letter is to give advice to my younger self, the truth is that I think it's my current self who could learn a thing or two from him. That ability to be fearless, to block out the noise from others, is something I've struggled to find at times over the last year in particular. I know it's still there, but it feels so far away sometimes. I still have faith in myself to know what the right decision is, but I've been guilty of being too afraid to act on it at times.

It's time to change that.

Love,
Conor

Dr Chris George
Doctor

A doctor's note to my younger self:

To the kid growing up who was overweight at school, stammered through most sentences, wore braces, had corrections for a painful curvature of the spine, never fitted in at school and was always picked last for the sports team: you are enough.

You are enough and you are loved immensely by all those around you.

As you grow and overcome these hurdles, these physical imperfections will fade but you will forever understand the value of kindness and that beauty cannot be seen from the outside.

This is your superpower, so embrace it and let it guide you through life.

You will learn, more often than you deserve, that people can be unkind at times. But resilience and strength are something that will shape and mould you into the incredible person you are becoming day by day.

You are enough and you are loved immensely by all those around you.

Letters to My Younger Queer Self

You've turned eighteen, life has not turned out quite how you planned and you experience your first major setback. No university offers and your dream of becoming a doctor seems pretty far-fetched at this point. But you believe in yourself because your experiences on the playground have taught you to stand back up and to dust yourself off.

Keep going and banging on every door, and believe me, one will open. I promise.

This is your doctor's note. Your official sign-off to be exactly who you need to be. You. Yourself. You are enough.

Regards,

Your Future Self, Who is Now a Doctor

Suzi Ruffell

Comedian
Lesbian – She/Her

Hi Suzi,

   This is grown-up Suzi. Weird, right?!

I'm imagining you sitting on the 25, in a bottle-green uniform, a tight ponytail, school tie exquisitely knotted, neat. Ready for another day where time feels slower than usual. I think about you often, Little Suz – is that sweet or narcissistic? (That means self-involved.) I think about the stress and the shame that clouded our teen years. The desperation, the fear. I wish you could see us now, right this minute: it's 6.30 a.m. on a Thursday, I'm drinking tea (we still drink a lot of tea), I'm sat in the front room – it's recently been decorated, it looks great. Out the window I can see Brighton slowly waking up, lights turn on in windows, buses coming down the hill, the distant hum of a train taking commuters on their way. I like this time of day – getting up this early feels like cheating, like I've an extra slice of the day. I thought about writing you an epic letter, a memorandum on how to live this life. But then, I wondered, would it change the life we have? And I really don't want to do that. We have got to exactly where we want to be. A directive from the future might hinder it. So instead, some advice. From me to you, or rather, from me to me:

- Don't stress about how much you think about Mel C and Kate Winslet.
- Try harder at school – yes, some of the teachers are wankers, they really are, but take in as much as you can.
- Stop bunking off! Taking off your tie doesn't make you look like a businesswoman off to work, it makes you look like a 14-year-old in her school uniform without her tie. You're fooling no one, kiddo!
- Read more. Reading will become such a big part of your life. Writing will as well, which I know is a surprise. Allow yourself to fall into new worlds through novels. It doesn't matter how long it takes you to read them, don't feel embarrassed about it. No one's timing you, you're the only one who knows, doughnut!
- Our dyslexia will become a strength: you will realise your brain works a bit differently to other people in lots of ways. It will help your creativity. Don't shy away from it.

Letters to My Younger Queer Self

- Never order a bottle of wine after 1 a.m. – it won't feel good in the morning.
- You will find a job you love, adore even. But it won't be easy. Remember that it's OK to fail. It's OK to get things wrong. Perfection doesn't actually exist and generally people who seem perfect are very, very dull. We've always been in a rush to get to the finish line or achieve our goals. That's actually a really exhausting way to live. It's so cliché to say this but try and enjoy the journey. Force yourself to get off the train occasionally and have some fun, enjoy the view.
- Don't get a perm.
- You will make great friends, who really know you and love you. Remember birthdays, send cards and flowers. Remember to make them feel special. Send letters – everyone loves post that isn't a bill.
- I know, you know this, but you are a lesbian. We are gay and working that out is going to be brutal. Coming out will feel insurmountable but it isn't, you'll manage it. You don't need to rush it. It'll take you years to fully accept it, even though you'll do a good job of pretending you're fine while dancing on podiums in various clubs around Soho. Unlearning both society's and your own internalised homophobia will be a journey. You'll obsess about being the 'right' sort of gay, one that doesn't offend

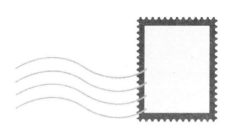

Send letters — everyone loves post that isn't a bill.

or irritate and slots easily into a heteronormative world. Eventually you'll think 'Fuck that!', which will be very freeing.
- Mum, Dad, Nan and the whole of the family will accept you, fully, with buckets of love, but do remember people's first reaction isn't always their best. Give them a chance to have a second one.
- Have a night in occasionally. Cook some proper food and go to bed early.
- You will fall in love.
- You will also get your heart broken, a couple of times. One of them is a real howler. You'll feel like you won't survive it, but you will. In fact, you'll learn more about yourself in that period than in any other. But to be clear, it'll hurt like hell.
- Going peroxide blonde will ruin your hair but I know you're going to do it anyway – just make sure they use a toner.
- The family you dream of isn't make-believe, it isn't a fantasy. It's possible, it will exist. In fact, upstairs still asleep is the greatest love we could imagine, a wife and a daughter who bring more joy than you believe is possible. Which I know feels unimaginable, unthinkable, impossible right now. But it will happen!

- Look after your body. Go to Pilates. I know it's a bit boring, but it's very good for you.
- Carry on trying to make everyone laugh – that'll come in useful one day.

Love,
Big Suz

Robert Diament

Gallerist and Podcaster – Talk Art
Gay
He/Him

Dear Robert,

I write to you from September in the year 2024. It's thirty years since Andrew died and I'm writing to let you know you will be OK. You will survive this. I know right now you're feeling very alone, isolated, sat in the bath trying to keep warm, trying to wash away the shock – the cold, cold shock – that your brother, your best friend – and the life you have known up until this point – is gone.

I remember that sinking feeling, the panic, that gigantic fear of being outed and the devastating knowledge that our parents would now likely never have grandchildren; that brutal realisation as a gay 13-year-old, about to turn fourteen, as you sit in the bath, that you may never have children, or even find someone to love you.

That you will never see your brother again. The very real likelihood that you won't even be alive very long yourself. The fear instilled within you since early childhood of being an outcast. The shame from knowing you are different to the other boys and the threat of an imminent death perhaps from a violent gay bashing, if people discover who you really are, or the visceral reality of AIDS on the horizon: your acute awareness of the stories of mass loss from a generation of gay men in the decade before.

As you grow into adulthood, you will build up emotional walls to protect yourself. You'll push love away, you'll go out into the world wearing a suit of armour – in order to survive – in an attempt never to let anyone hurt you again. But you will – and you must – get hurt. Your heart will – and must – be broken. And you will despair. You will even lose more family, some friends, young and old, but the most powerful lesson you will learn through all of this is to stay as open as you can.

Fall in love, be vulnerable, risk getting hurt. Never forget that underneath your steely shell is the soft you, the gentle you, the you with an open heart. You have a big capacity for love. Eventually you will learn that your heart is one that has no fear of love, of intimate connection. Your heart is one of limitless possibility.

Think back to your 4-year-old self, obsessed with dancing and ballet – and even with the sculptural form of the ballet shoe?! Your infinite joy and passion for creating a brand-new dance routine from scratch. That rush of creativity, of birthing a new idea. Singing, acting, writing hundreds of songs on the piano, writing poem after poem, or recording make-believe interviews on your tape recorder as an imaginary radio DJ. Play and creativity are something you always had, since you drew your first breath, something you need and are fuelled by. They will never leave you, they will never let you down.

You may not see this yet but you have a superpower: your ability to connect to others, to seek out love, to give love, and eventually, all roads will lead you to creativity and to art. You will find a world where you can nurture others and they will nurture you, and you will find loyal, intimate, loving friendships.

Cry if you need to cry. Feel everything you can feel, to its upmost intensity, but always remember to try and get some sleep. Remember that when you wake up in the morning, everything will feel lighter. Tomorrow is never as bad as you anticipate. Stay focused. Stay passionate. Stay truthful and, most of all, make friends with yourself. Be kind to yourself. Liking yourself is harder than it sounds but when you begin to finally get closer to this goal, a contentment will arrive that will make you realise you're not that bad after all. It's OK to be you and I promise you this – one day you'll be really proud of yourself. You have a strength deep within you that you

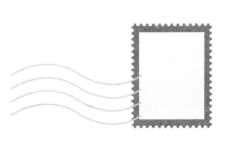

Fall in love, be vulnerable, risk getting hurt.

can summon anytime you need. You can always rely on yourself – your conviction, your drive, your work ethic, your big dreams, your curiosity, your desire to connect and reach out to people all across the world. Your wish to help others feel less alone. One day you'll achieve it but in a way you never expected. Sometimes the things that come easiest to us are the ones we suppress but you will learn that what comes easy is often your greatest power! The skills we spend years not utilising, once unlocked, will help you fulfil an immense potential.

As you look out of your bathroom skylight, with the door locked, sitting on the carpeted floor fixating through the early hours at the gold moon high above, you are right in believing that somewhere out there is a place for you. There are people just like you, looking at the same moon, in this very same moment, dreaming of being free.

Now, go to sleep.

X

All best,
Robert

Ryan Lanji

TV Personality
Gay
He/Him

Oh, Little Lanji,

What a titan you are – a rocket full of flamboyant energy, with colours bursting out from every seam of your being. Look at you, with your wide eyes and wild imagination, already rebelling against the dullness of the world around you. You're a star in your own right, a constellation in the making, even if the sky doesn't yet know how to hold you.

I know how hard it is to feel like you're too much in a world that constantly tells you to be less. But here's a secret: you're not too much, they're just not ready. Your queerness is a force, not a flaw. It's the engine that will drive you to places you can't even imagine right now, to people who will see you, love you, and celebrate every inch of who you are. You're not just a dancer in life's masquerade, darling – you're the one designing the costumes.

And yes, I know. I know what it feels like to be South Asian and queer, to carry the weight of cultures and expectations on your shoulders, always wondering if there's a space where both parts of you can coexist without compromise. But Little Lanji, you will find that place. One day, you will pack up your courage and head to London, a city teeming with possibilities, a city that doesn't just tolerate difference but thrives on it.

London will be the canvas for your dreams. You'll arrive unsure, a little scared, but oh-so-ready to make some noise. You'll find your tribe – other queer South Asians who know exactly what it's like to live on the fringes, to rewrite the rules. Together, you'll carve out spaces where you don't just belong – you reign. You'll host parties that become legendary, create communities where people feel seen, celebrated and safe.

You'll accomplish things you never thought possible – becoming a voice for the voiceless, an advocate for those who felt too afraid to dance to their own beat. You'll change the very fabric of your world, Little Lanji. You'll do it by being unapologetically yourself, by loving fiercely and by refusing to let anyone dim the light you've been given.

There will be days when you'll feel like you're spinning, out of sync with everyone else. Days when you'll wonder if it would just be easier to blend in. Don't.

There will be days when you'll feel like you're spinning, out of sync with everyone else. Days when you'll wonder if it would just be easier to blend in. Don't. Blend. In. Every single shade, every flick of your wrist, every time you speak up or laugh too loud or love too fiercely, you are painting a world where all of us can breathe a little easier.

Blend. In. Every single shade, every flick of your wrist, every time you speak up or laugh too loud or love too fiercely, you are painting a world where all of us can breathe a little easier.

You're a trailblazer, even when you don't feel like one. You're paving paths for others who, like you, feel that they don't belong anywhere because they belong everywhere. You'll be a beacon, a voice, a living, breathing protest that declares: I am here and I refuse to be anything less than myself.

So, keep sashaying down those streets with your head held high, shoulders back and heart open. You're going to light up rooms, darling, even when they don't have a clue how to handle your wattage. And someday, you'll help make this world just a little bit brighter, a little bit kinder, a little bit queerer.

Celebrate your magic. Your unapologetic spirit is your gift to the world – never forget that. And remember, there's a whole community of us out here, dancing alongside you, waiting for you to come into your own, rooting for you every step of the way.

With love and all the glitter you can carry,
Your Future Self

A Letter of Complaint ...
To Our Education System

Trigger warning: Suicide

To Whom It May Concern,

I'd like to register a complaint. I'm writing from a place of trepidation for all children under this educational authority.

I realise there are multiple barriers within the education system. Constant cuts being made and teachers' time already being spread thinly. But you have a very important job to do and when it comes to preparing the youth of today, I'm afraid to say, as a society, you are failing them.

I'm writing to complain about the lack of information provided to our youth. Are you preparing them for their lives? Really? I'm not talking about teaching equations and the periodic table to understand the world, though this calculation that I'm presented with is clear to me. It's an easy sum to crack. I'm talking about the other preparation they require to understand their place in it. The nurturing of who they are, or who they might become. The information they might need.

Can you wholeheartedly say that your sex education caters wider than a heterosexual example of what might come? Are your children learning about the huge advances in medicine and the impact PrEP is having on a community that was at the centre of an AIDS witch hunt? Well? Do your children know that sex can look very different dependent on your preferences, orientation or feelings? Are they aware that porn is not the example of what's to come? Have you told them that sex can be painful or messy? And, for some ... they might not even ever want it.

That's OK, is it?

Have you also explained to the boys that it's OK if you go soft occasionally? Lose your hard-on before or during? That it happens to us all? Far more often than we might realise. Please do that, it might help them later in understanding and not feeling so bloody alone. I apologise for the tone, but it's frustrating not to have that knowledge, wouldn't you agree? To be able to feel 'normal' in a world where it's hard to know what that word even means.

Are you reassuring your children? Are you supporting the boy who wears the dress, protecting him from the bully that has issues he's yet to realise himself? Are you teaching them about genders far and wide from what we ourselves might have suffered in school? From the blue and the pink? From those lessons we sat in and pondered, confused, about where we fitted in. If we fitted in? We didn't fit in. The awkward swelling inside of us worrying that we'll walk out of school and into a world that we don't understand and doesn't know us back. The job you have to prepare them ... Have you done it? Truly?

Are your trans students safe? Have you asked them how they are? Do you normalise them, encourage their talent? Are you treating them equally? Supporting them? Do not ever use the term 'kids will be kids' – they won't. They can be bastards and you bloody well know it. But they can also be adults. They can have knowledge. They can grow under your watch. It's not just down to the parents – you know that, right?

Are you, yourself, accepting everyone? Honestly? It's OK not to fully understand things yourself. It's also OK not to know the answer to that question. But are you willing to try? Are you willing to let your students teach you something?

Do the girls in your classrooms feel inspired to break glass ceilings? To be more than a role from a dated time, way back when? Are you giving them a fair chance at the race of life? I wonder if they know about choice, about feelings and worries – and how to speak up, use their voices. They should. They are important. Equal. They need to know far more than just what a tampon is and where it goes. When you teach them about reproduction, are you also sharing that it's OK if you choose not to have children? That they won't be an outcast or a 'freak' if they choose to be childless and happy with that choice? Have you told them about the commonality of miscarriages? Freezing eggs? The pain of labour?

I'm writing out of concern.

You have failed so many children already, you need to pull your socks up. Because, educators, it really does start with you. You are the voice in the classroom that can normalise the 'odd', the 'weak', the 'queer'. You can make lives better. You can save lives. You literally have every walk of life and difference at your fingertips. To nurture. Don't turn a blind eye to things that you don't understand. Educating someone is also about educating yourself. Come on now, you know full well we don't stop learning after we leave the dangerous school corridors. It never stops – it shouldn't ever stop.

I'm writing to say that it's not too late to right a wrong – a wrong by so many looking back at their education. Are you doing better than your teachers? I'm writing to encourage you to look past the 'basics' that we might need and think what might have helped someone on the outskirts, someone not relating to the curriculum you are currently spouting.

Are you doing all that you can?

Letters to My Younger Queer Self

You've come a long way, but there are many miles to travel and I need to know that you're up to the task. Up for the journey ahead? You have a very important job, and, frankly, you CANNOT fail. There are lives that need you and that won't survive without your knowledge. You owe them that information. I cannot read about another suicide, another lost soul, another child that wasn't helped in areas they needed it most. An unprepared casualty of life.

Educators, I know that you have a battle on your hands and I applaud you for going into this war, but this is a war you can win. With tools and knowledge, it's a fight that can be won. I know there are plenty of grey areas in a sea of rainbows. Paths that if you tread them can get you in foreign waters, but you can help, even if it's just a little bit more than what you've already done.

Please register this formal complaint for a past failure and make a mend for a future you can save. Please listen. Please educate. Please support.

Sincerely,
An outcast who wasn't prepared

Conclusion: Signed, Sealed, Delivered

Dear Reader ...

... and so, I ask you, have you ever received a letter? Not a bank statement, bill, flyer or abandoned Amazon delivery note, but an actual letter, written with heart or meaning? The answer is most likely yes, I hope. But perhaps not always when you needed it the most. An out-of-the-blue piece of advice or note that could change your mood, or better, your life.

Well, these are for you to keep and return to when you need them most.

A letter, in this collection from a wonderful group of people, might not alter anything. It might not change your future, narrative, or even your mind. It might make you smile, or laugh or cry; it might even provoke a thought on your own journey that lies ahead. But imagine the power the letter may have had when you were struggling. When you were at your darkest, lowest, or just wanted to know it will be OK. Those letters could be just the sign you need to pull through. To be reminded that you are enough, and that you are not alone.

Without these tests, fights, fears or loves, we wouldn't be us. We would not be the *us* that we are today – and *we* are all amazing. Each and every one of our rainbow acronym.

Not too long ago, I met a man and had a whirlwind romance on holiday. During a moment together, he told me that he loves to write letters. Handwritten notes, even a postcard. I asked him, why? He told me, 'There is an intimacy in a handwritten note that doesn't exist in our electronic world.'

When you put pen to paper, realness comes out and perhaps even more thought than you ever imagined. Something that you were unaware of that you needed to convey. We should never stop writing. And so, in our electronic world, these are a gift to you.

These incredible, beautiful, heartfelt letters give a snapshot of our ever-expanding community. These writers have shown themselves in their most raw, vulnerable light, in the hope that someone – perhaps sitting at home, scared, alone or even surrounded by others – might read one letter from this book that gives them a glimmer of who they are, or who they might be. Who they feel they could be deep down inside. Because when life gives us letters, we should accept them. And the beauty of those special words, written down for you, is that it can be read again and again, and as many times as you need. Best accompanied by a cup of coffee or a Cosmopolitan.

I leave you with this final letter and thought: Is there someone, somewhere, who needs your words? Well then, please pick up a pen and give them the best possible gift.

Yours truly,
Daniel x

P.S. To all younger people, you too will feel old one day. Remember that.

Notes on my fridge now

- Love yourself
- Vote
- Be kind
- Protect Trans children
- All LGBTQIA+ people are legal and seen

Charities

Every important letter within this book represents a donation to two fantastic charities who support our community and the importance of our mental health, journeys and paths. We thank you.

MindOut
MindOut is a mental health service run by and for lesbians, gay, bisexual, trans and queer people. We work to improve the mental wellbeing of LGBTQIA+ communities and to make mental health a community concern. Our vision is a world where the mental health of LGBTQIA+ communities is a priority, free from stigma, respected and recognised.

Just Like Us
Just Like Us is the LGBTQIA+ young people's charity. Growing up LGBTQIA+ is still unacceptably tough. Just Like Us works with thousands of primary and secondary schools as well as young people across the UK to ensure LGBTQIA+ young people can thrive.

Letters to My Younger Queer Self

The charity provides free resources as well as Pride Groups, talks to schools and supports LGBTQIA+ young people with career mentoring, volunteering training and more.

Support and Helplines

Please see below a list of charities and organisations that could help with any themes discussed within these letters. You will find helplines listed on their websites:

AKT – www.akt.org.uk
Alcoholics Anonymous – www.alcoholics-anonymous.org.uk
Alcohol Change – alcoholchange.org.uk
Body Dysmorphic Disorder Foundation – bddfoundation.org
IMARA – imara.org.uk
Just Like Us – www.justlikeus.org
LGBT Foundation – lgbt.foundation
Mind – www.mind.org.uk/
MindOut – mindout.org.uk
National AIDS Trust – www.nat.org.uk
National Domestic Abuse Helpline – www.nationaldahelpline.org.uk
Not A Phase – notaphase.org
Rainbow Noir – www.rainbownoirmcr.com
Refuge – refuge.org.uk
Safeline – safeline.org.uk
Samaritans – www.samaritans.org
Stonewall – www.stonewall.org.uk
Terrence Higgins Trust – www.tht.org.uk/

Acknowledgements

A massive and heartfelt thank you to everyone who has contributed to this book. From the letters you've read to the conversations I've had around them and the inspiration they have sparked. It's been a beautiful and important process. Huge thanks to Mum, Dad, Debbie and Laura, my family and friends, forever supporting all of our unique letters. And my sister especially, for putting up with my 'writer's mood' at times. To my incredible publishing team at HarperCollins for all their work and advice, and my agent Andrew at Frog.

And special thanks to:

Alaska, Stu Oakley, Lotte Jeffs, Dr Chris George, Ryan Lanji, Conor Clark, Alexandra Blyth Sharman Cox, Louise Jones, Mark Whittam, Nadia Whittome, James Barr, Suzi Ruffell, Ella Morgan, Sean Saifa Wall, Mix Stress – Rebecca Swarray, Andrew Donaldson-Wheatcroft, Andrew Stamp, Sarah Savage, Tom Aspaul, Adam Theo, Alastair James, Shivani Dave, Anita Wigl'it AKA Nick, Philip Baldwin, Dr James Greenwood, Radam Ridwan, Calum McSwiggan, David Atherton, Onairplanemode – Christine Diaz and Kirstie Pike,

Letters to My Younger Queer Self

Jamie Windust, Ben Pechey, Paris Munro, Dave Cooper, James Longman, Alysse Dalessandro, Charlotte Minett, Cyrill Ibrahim, Robert Diament, Bright Light Bright Light – Rod, Ashley Moran, Cody Daigle-Orians, Hafsa Qureshi, Paul Davies, Michael Perry and Adrien Gaubert.

A gorgeous and important bunch of letters in our beautiful acronym.